Marius Bewley — 1957

EZRA POUND AND THE CANTOS

EZRA POUND

and

THE CANTOS

by

HAROLD H. WATTS

CHICAGO
HENRY REGNERY COMPANY
1952

PRINTED IN GREAT BRITAIN
BY W & J. MACKAY & CO., LTD., CHATHAM

CONTENTS

MR. POUND'S PILGRIMAGE

S INCE, at least, the time of Van Wyck Brooks' *The Pilgrimage of Henry James*, it is conventional to apply the key-term *pilgrimage* to American writers who withdraw from what is called 'the American scene' and take up residence in alien regions. Certainly in this very simple sense, Ezra Pound *is* a pilgrim. Starting out in Colorado, the son of a government mining assayer, with stops at Hamilton College, the University of Pennsylvania, London, Paris, and Venice, Pound finally arrived at Rapallo, a small Italian town not far from Genoa. There, up to the time of the second World War, Pound continued an existence that was not nearly so obscure as his own sense of neglect suggested to him. After Italy's entrance into the war, Pound's broadcasts from the country of his exile removed all odium of obscurity. Still an American citizen, he was named a traitor to his country; the National Institute of Arts and Letters was urged to expel him (but did not); and after his arrest, he was brought back to this country and escaped trial by being adjudged a mental case.

Doubtless the discovery that Pound was not able to stand trial was—as well as being a fact—a convenient 'out' for those who were handling *l'affaire Pound*. For if he is not mentally sound, persons in authority will not have to draw up with care the case against him. They will not have to inspect and weigh the ideas that led to Pound's broadcasts (broadcasts which the Justice Department described as 'rantings and ravings'; broadcasts for which—the indictment ran—Pound received payment). The ideas involved in such broadcasts are ideas that Pound for many years expressed in prose and verse: verse that a conventional publishing house thought it creditable to issue, prose that received the imprimatur of the Yale University Press. Naturally, neither the publishing house nor the Yale University Press is involved in Pound's 'case'; but Pound's war-time gestures are intelligible only to the person who has studied *The Cantos* and Pound's essays on the art of reading and culture.

Perhaps, as with Henry James's 'pilgrimage', the real import of Pound's journey is grasped only superficially if one regards it as a journey in space, from Colorado to Italy. Such a journey is chiefly quaint. The real journey, the real pilgrimage, consisted of certain rather devious travels taken in time, and it can be maintained that Pound's war-time broadcasts were the culmination of these particular journeys. Similarly, James's assumption of English citizenship ended a life-long exploration of alternatives; his act asserted which alternative pleased him. So did Pound's. Both acts were—hasty judgment would put it—rejections of America. With James, at least, this snap judgment no longer 'washes'; he had to become a British citizen because he had explored to their limits certain American possibilities: the development of individual taste in esthetic and moral matters. When the America of 1914 seemed to him indifferent to the struggle in Europe, a struggle in which Kultur was pitted against civilization (indeed, what was civilization but a collection of chances to refine upon one's individual apprehensions?), James detached himself from America. He had not failed America; America had, in his judgment, failed him.

Pound's 'case' is also made up of an intellectual journey that ends in an act, a profession of faith. Even if Pound did indeed receive payment for his services, his broadcasts had very little in common with the Nazi-supervised air-talks of 'Lord Haw-Haw' and others. These latter betrayals were reduced by Rebecca West to simple psychoses of which the component parts were family wrangles and emotional deficiencies; such traitors can be handled with condescending pity. There is little to pity in Pound; there is a good deal to comprehend. The experts have tried to tell us what Pound's psychoses are; according to one, Pound is now 'in a paranoic state of psychotic proportions which renders him unfit for trial', and another observer remarks that he cannot reason coherently. But to lean heavily on these reports is a kind of evasion; we escape asking what, for us, is the total import of *The Cantos*, the speculation in prose, and (of course) the treason. What Pound has done is much more than the expression of a psychosis; it is more than a malformation of personality that can have only clinical interest. Rather, as with James, Pound's act was the fruition of a series of choices and judgments made over a period of many years: choices and judgments that we cannot be indifferent to unless we are indifferent to choices and judgments that we ourselves must make.

Not that Pound's choices are devoid of elements that can be called personal. Deep-cutting was the neglect and lack of comprehension from the English-speaking world. But it is too easy a solution to write off Pound's broadcasts from Italy as the expression of pique. Pique is at work;

but much more than pique found expression. It is this 'much more' that Pound's judges—judicial and literary—must look at.

II

This 'much more' would be unlikely to exist if Pound had not begun by being, by birth and by formal education, an American. As Eliot says of James, it is only an American who can choose to be a European. And, of course, there are several sorts of Europeans to choose to be. Pound, in his thought, has achieved a certain sort of detachment from American, but this detachment should not be identified as Left-bankism or art-snobbery. It is, in fact, a detachment made in the name of humane values that dominated the minds of the American founding fathers—values that have since been pushed into the background of American life, recognized as inoperative 'h'ants' that are unlikely to alter the course followed by American culture. A formula that Pound often quotes is this one of Jefferson's; Freedom is the exercise of liberty that does not interfere with the liberty of others. In a century and a half, American history has (some would argue) altered that formula to this one: Freedom is the exercise of liberty, whether or not it interferes with the rights of others. In Pound's view, at any rate, democracy in America has undergone decay and lives on as capitalist-democracy, something that Jefferson would have detested. It is the destruction of capitalist-democracy that, with the passing of the years, Pound grew to hope for. One should recognize that this hope was—in part, at least—instructed by the initial promises of democracy itself.

But only in part. For this hope of Pound's has found nourishment elsewhere. Later we shall ask what is the relationship between this composite hope and his broadcasts.

Pound's mental pilgrimage can be divided into two stages. Pound, now a man of advanced years, left America in the first decade of this century. Life was not possible there on his terms. Liberty to do what he wished (compose poetry, immerse himself in the cultures of times chosen and distant, all 'without harm' to others) conflicted with liberty as, apparently, it was understood: this was a more restricted liberty that permitted one to do only those things that were not inimical to the *status quo* as it had been established, a *status quo* which favoured the making of fortunes in speculation and certainly a far cry from what Pound (and Jefferson and John Adams and a good many others) regarded as the life-giving essence of a democracy. Such a culture, capitalist-democratic culture, would have little tolerance for the creation of excellence and the admiration of excellence (the two motives have told equally with Pound). Pound went to England and lived there several years. But unlike Henry James and the later great Anglophile, T. S. Eliot, Pound found nothing to tie him to the island. He bent his steps to the continent; nor did he pause long on the Left Bank. One might say that, by the time of the first World War, America and England had taught him what to hate. At the same time, he had been learning what to love from his studies of past cultures (Greek, Provencal, and Chinese are the ranking ones for Pound).

The second stage of his mental pilgrimage—the two decades that preceded 1940—were, as already noted, spent chiefly at Rapallo: a town that, because of its magnificent view of the sea, has drawn such other famous visitors as Nietzsche and W. B. Yeats. The reasons for Pound's prolonged stay are complex. But his own comment makes clear that existence at Rapallo was more than possible; it was good. ('Italy,' Pound told ship reporters in 1939, 'is the seat of culture in the Occident.') Pound dated his later writings by the years of the Fascist regime; for it had provided him with the good life—or a closer approximation to that life than America or England permitted him to make. Further, from his eyries on the Mediterranean, he found it easy to transfix England and America, regions never for long escaping his study. Indeed, a large part of his sense of intellectual well-being came from noting frequently what it was that he had put behind him.

Several aids clarify, for Pound, the great distance between Rapallo and the Anglo-Saxon countries, the eminence of the goal he had reached. They are, in order of ascending strangeness to us, these: Italian life (its permanent texture apart from the Fascist additions); aspects of the history of the Catholic Church; the theories of certain economists, in themselves and in what Pound judges to be their partial realization in the Italian Fascist state.

Italian life, in its permanent texture, need not detain us; for it has for Pound merits which several other Anglo-Saxon writers have made out. That life is natural and direct; it is not tyrannized over by the organizing and systematic hypocrisy of Anglo-Saxon countries. And centuries ago the Catholic Church in Italy (not elsewhere, in Pound's view) made its peace with paganism so that, one may say, every Madonna is a Venus slightly transmogrified. Thus, in Italy, natural man can remain natural; he need not compress himself into moulds that are no creations of nature, that are the creations (in our era) of the most anti-natural human activity: the making of fortunes by the taking of interest and rent.

In many great periods of history, we can notice (with

guidance from Pound) that the lending of money for interest was not tolerated; for a healthy society will feel that the lending of money, the piling up of wealth on the basis of interest or rent, is against nature and against the good of collective man. (Pound here follows—or selects from—such economists as C. H. Douglas and Silvio Gesell.) Payment for produce and for hours of expended labour has always been payment for a reality. Payment for use of money is, instead, payment for a service that is sterile, that does not ever add to the sum-total of natural goods. Further—and this is one of the chief sins of capitalist-democracy in Pound's view—when a bank creates credit that outruns its actual assets (brutally, the money actually put in its coffers), it takes over—in fact, if not technically—one of the chief functions of the state: the issue and control of coinage. (The same sin is committed by those who over-finance a corporation.) In short, what seems to many an economist orthodox modern practice is, in the view of Pound and the economists he has taken for his teachers, a thinly veiled robbery. For an increase of money—or its equivalents, credit or stock—without a precisely corresponding increase of goods available for purchase acts to debase each unit of money. If there is no more produce actually available for purchase, it is certain that the purchasing power of a coin wanes, and along with it the security of the man whose physical comfort, whose freedom to create and to admire what great past cultures have created was once adequately assured by his income. A fixed income worked, in non-capitalistic cultures, no unpredictable hardships; a fixed income is to-day subject to sudden expansions and diminutions of credit, to stupefying hardships. And that is not all the darkness which Pound—fortified by the natural goodness of life in Italy—sees along Wall and

Threadneedle Streets. The subtle tactics of high finance—manœuvred by monstrous, pustulent creatures that (Pound promises in *The Cantos*) will end up in a malodorous hell—tend to dissolve the authority that real property once had over men's imaginations. No longer does man work to get his own vine and fig-tree; gilt-edged, interest-bearing bonds are a better protection against wind and weather.

All this—which Pound lumps together under the term of abuse: usury—is close-linked, in Pound's history, with the very sterilities and avoidances that drove him to Italy. Let us be sure to see what this link is. Ordinarily, the fair estate of poetry is a topic that (to the conventional man of our 'capitalistic-democratic' culture) seems perfectly safe. True, it is not one that he ever brings up at his luncheon club; but those who do—in his hearing, in his chance reading—are useless but harmless fellows: a different company from those disturbing persons who write of socialism and undermine the American way of life and the First National Bank. A careless view of Pound sees him as an accidental composition of these two types: the harmless propagandist for poetry, the sinister champion of an un-American, totalitarian régime—in short, a poet who happens to have treasonable economic and political theories. Pound's view of his own thought cancels the verb *happens*; for him, the empowering words are *must have*. He is a poet who must—*because* he is a poet—take a dark view of capitalistic democracy, of (more briefly) usury.

To perceive all this—to see that the link between Pound's stance as a poet and critic of poetry and as a vilifier of the country of which he is a citizen—is to see how, in Pound's view, usury is the enemy of poetry in our time as well as the bitter foe of all other natural human goods.

The best way to grasp this link is to note what Pound's

tableau of poetic greatness is. It includes Homer, certain
Greek lyrists, the Provencal singers, the Italians Cavalcanti and Dante, the English Donne, and (roughly) the
French symbolists. (Pound *thinks* it would include the classic
Chinese collections of Odes were he master of Chinese.)
The table excludes Vergil, Milton, and all the famous poetry
of nineteenth century English literature as taught in survey
courses at American 'learneries' (Pound's phrase). Scruti-
nizing the backgrounds against which great poems appear,
Pound often makes out that the social and economic patterns
of these times either favoured the making of great poetry
or, at any rate, did not place insuperable barriers across the
poet's path—did not (to vary the figure) generate an in-
sidious miasma that the poet of less happy ages must
breathe, that (for example) to-day's poet breathes without
suspecting that every expansion of his lungs draws in air
that undermines his poetic line and his handling of the
language he was born to. Such a poet becomes a writer
with whom usury has no quarrel, for he uses the language
facilely and uncritically. But usury must live in horrid
fear of poets who use the language well—use it with
incision, with a perdurable consciousness that words can
be more than a dough, can be instruments to expose and
to cut away diseased tissue. Thus, the Victorian capitalist
had nothing to fear from the poetry that his lovely daughter
read beside the fire. The 'romantic' poet did no more than
bandy between himself and his reader vague abstractions
that were no real threat to the *status quo*. No one was going
to put those abstractions to the test and find out what they
meant *in action*. Certainly the poets would not, nor would
the lovely reader at her fireside. As Pound sees it, when
Dante inveighs against usury, he is a dangerous fellow;
but when Shelley hymns the brotherhood of mortals, when

Wordsworth urges on the reader the need for mergings with nature, either poet remains a household pet—frolicsome but not likely to smash more than a teacup. (Objections to this contrast may occur to the reader of this essay, but they do not occur to Pound.)

And it is as household pets that poets and their art must exist (Pound argues) in a capitalist-democracy. Any poet, any person, who wishes to go against the current in our age, to 'make things new'—'make it new' is a key-phrase with Pound, one which he derives from a Chinese ideogram —will function as Dante functioned. He will be dangerous because his perceptive use of the language will destroy the quarter-truths or the outright fictions on which the prestige of usury—of what is more flatteringly called 'business enterprise' and 'business vision'—rests.

In some ages—Pound would teach us—the economic structure favoured, or at any rate did not make impossible, the utterance of insights prophetic or poetic within the shelter of the age. But in our age—democracy having become what it is, what John Adams to his horror foresaw, what Alexander Hamilton ('the biggest snot in *all* American history' Pound calls him) wished for—the poet must attack society as it is now constituted. He must rescue from its forums a language that has been debased by the uses it has been put to. He must seize away learning from the endowed —and thereby 'safe'—universities which usury has set up. He must also—since he must live in *some* society, since Pound's own studies do not encourage him, as many artists were once encouraged, to regard art as a thing independent of the social forms which surround it—seek out the societies in his own time that favour art or at least do not stultify it utterly.

To seek out such societies in times past is, of course,

easy for Pound. He singles out (in *The Cantos* as well as in his essays) the credit reforms in Siena in the early seventeenth century; he venerates Leopold of Hapsburg-Lorraine, who, by his credit legislation, made the Duchy of Tuscany a decent place in which to live until Napoleon came crashing down from France. But such societies, though they may serve as examples, cannot be substitutes —either for the poet or for the human beings dependent on the poet's insights—for actually seeking out a relatively good society in one's own era. For Pound there are—or were—two such societies: the Catholic Church and the Italian Fascist state.

Pound's mention of the Church may surprise in a day when anti-clericalism is the tone of much literature that is 'advanced'. Yet to explain this preference is to repeat, in explicit terms, the analysis just made of Pound's general attack on usury. Until the Renaissance, Pound judges, the Church was the enemy of usury. Later, it has at least insisted upon a distinction between interest (a small charge for the use of money) and usury (a large charge in the long run ruinous to everyone concerned). The Church has insisted on this distinction as Protestantism with its emphasis on individual paths to salvation has not. (Protestantism teaches that the Voice of God has the only right to censure usury; and doubtless that voice is drowned out in the Pit.) Further, though Pound is no friend of theology (it sinfully abstracts words from the life-stream that is reality), Catholic abstractions—unlike those to be encountered in 'romantic' poets—are precise in definition; they mean one thing and not ten vaguely related things. The poet (Pound, that is) cannot respect the conclusions of Aquinas; but he can respect his rigorous use of language. (In a usurious civilization nothing must be named precisely, for then the triumph of evil, the waste of virtue, would be correctly described.) Speaking of the totality of the Church, Pound observes that he could become a Catholic if he were allowed to pick his saints and teachers. For example, the papal encyclical *Quadragesimo Anno* is a respectable document. But, unfortunately, Pound's favourite Schoolman—Scotus Erigena, who taught, 'Authority has its basis in right reason'—has been declared a heretic; nor does the official Church recognize intellectually what for practical purposes it condones: the blending in Italy of antique paganism and Christianity.

So, for Pound in his search, one other present order remained: the Corporative State as it was being put together in Italy. Here, apparently, was authority that had its basis in right reason. Here, at least, was a corrective to capitalist-democracy. To Pound, Mussolini's reforms were all anti-usurious in intent: the tying-together of various industries having a common product, the limitation of private profit, the subordination of the 'drives' of separate industries to the needs of the state. The state was the reality that embraced all individuals, that worked toward giving them, in return for devotion, the 'realization' that, under capitalist-democracy, they could never have hoped for. Of course, Pound takes himself to be, at all turns of his career, an intellectual aristocrat; so he does not, in *any* social context, expect that enslaving devotion will be demanded of him. Further, he does not expect much in way of a 'making new' of the masses; at the most, they may participate—if distantly—in what can be accomplished by the individual poet under favourable conditions. Pound plainly saw the labour of Mussolini was the equivalent, on the political stage, of his own on the stage provided by language. (It is beside the point that Pound called the

Italian dictator, in retrospect, 'a puffed up bubble': he had failed to measure up to Pound's ideal expectations.) Both Mussolini and he had shrugged off the chains capitalist-democracy binds across the shoulders of vigorous men: men whose labours (if allowed to unfold, to burgeon) would be life-giving to the entire body-politic. The draining of the Pontine marches, the efforts of fascist economists to centre attention on realities (grain, wool, wheat) rather than on the paper canopies capitalistic economists patch together and then venerate, certain tax reforms of Mussolini's government—all these have Pound's approval. These changes are not—to employ a distinction that Pound is fond of—abstract ideas existing in the romantic inane and unlikely to alter the course followed by the stream of history; they are 'ideas in action' that record real application of the mind of the planner to reality, real dredging and conservations and consolidations. Here the link between Pound the political thinker and Pound the poet should be plain. Pound's own poetry puts—his hope is—words themselves to work again; and they are to work with reality and not abstractions, they are to work for the common good, they are an essential part of the programme of 'making things new.'

III

The book in which these ideas find fullest utterance is called *Culture*. It is a book that begins by seeming disjointed and rambling—as the psychologists tell us that Pound's speech now is. But Pound's book ends by being perfectly self-consistent—in fact, a work no more the creation of a madman than the somewhat less disjointed but still disorderly lucubrations of Montaigne and Rabelais. This treatise, along with the evidence to be found elsewhere, suggests that Pound's journey to Rapallo was made in the name of a great variety of human goods—as William James would say, a plurality of goods. Many of these goods, though not all, were human values that the founding fathers were not indifferent to. It is a fact that Pound's strictures upon capitalist-democracy, his estimate of the position of poetry in England and America, and numerous ancillary remarks do not strike one as entirely novel. They were, indeed, voiced by many people in England and America previous to 1940 and still found expression in this country during the years of actual warfare when publicists desired to remind us of what democracy could be and ought to become.

What, if anything, distinguishes the position of Pound from that of many respected, home-dwelling Americans? Certainly not what his spirit urges him to bear witness *against* in democracy-as-is. He arrived at what can be described as an attitude of treason by dwelling on certain suppositions which blocked out for him potentialities that others, remaining at home, still found in modern democracy —potentialities which he has not for decades found in 'Anglo-Saxondom'. This same intransigent emphasis enabled Pound to perceive, in Fascist Italy, a promise of human good that other observers did not see. Specifically, he supposed that America was irremediably Wall Street's; and, despite preliminary warmth for the New Deal, he came to regard it as one more *pis aller* which Wall Street tolerated if it did not encourage. Regeneration of humanity, of a political and economic sort, would have to come from elsewhere. And where, in the Western world, might that happy region be if not in Fascist Italy? Most American and British students of the Fascist regime distinguish between economic and fiscal reforms as put on paper and their actual halting realization; and they find the gap very wide—so wide that only war, only distracting activity and the fruits of victory could conceal from outsiders and from observant Italians this truth: though the framework of the Italian state was altered, the degree of human security, the level of artistic excellence remained much what they were previous to 1922. Pound—such was his passion, such his hope—minimized the breakdowns, exaggerated the achievements (as, in another context, 'fellow-travellers' did), and blandly ignored the cruelty that was actually (if not of necessity) a contributing element to what success there was.

When Pound's case is reviewed—'when and if', in legal idiom—the history of opinion we have just summarized is the crucial evidence rather than the depositions of those who saw Pound prepare recordings for re-broadcast and the vouchers indicating what he was paid. Raising one's voice against democracy—against our failure to realize the promise implicit in a set of ideas—is an old habit in America; no man, in ordinary times, is sent to Leavenworth for expression of a passionate devotion to the unrealized ideals of our origin. But Pound's was a voice out of season; and his choice of context was lamentable. Doubtless his attacks gave 'aid and comfort to an enemy'. (His utterance —for weal or woe—had no impact whatever here.) But it is well to distinguish between two associated acts of judgment on Pound's part: what will seem to many the optimistic naiveté which permitted him to believe that his general hopes found specification in Fascist Italy; and what remains for many—or we should hope remains for many —the need of striving toward (as Pound strove) an inclusive view of the goods that civilized life has presented man in various ages, a clear view of the conditions under which those goods were realized and might be realized again.

IV

It is Pound's effort to draw up—in his studies and in his poetry—an inclusive view that gives him a strong claim on our present attention. It is an effort that few persons would call treasonable. But we must avoid entertaining—if only in the back of our minds—the impression that Pound's struggle for an inclusive view can be shorn of its political connections. Ever since certain modern writers on economic questions helped Pound to see the light, the writer of *The Cantos* would have rejected the label that Thomas Mann once wore with some smugness, as a thinker and artist: the label that proclaims that the creator is and should be an 'unpolitical man'. As we shall see, Pound kept unwaveringly before him the conviction that the poet is essentially a political animal—not just because he is a man but because he is a poet. Most *men* (Pound's aristocratic insight suggests) are too intellectually torpid, too deeply engrossed in the problems of survival, to be political at all—that is, to discover and master some coign of vantage from which they can look at the society in which they live. Rather must ordinary men rely upon the struggles of that political animal par excellence, the poet. It is he who—by study and by direct exercise of his art—discovers the merit of past cultures, and works to make that merit viable in our present lamentable one.

Thus stated in general terms, this claim for the poet is not novel. (Did not Shelley—whom Pound detests—write that poets are the unacknowledged legislators of the world?) What is novel in the phenomenon we call 'Pound' (his overt acts, his researches, *The Cantos*) is the very definite limitation he places on the activity of the poet as political animal, his harsh reduction in number of the conditions under which that activity can be in any way useful to modern society.

To perceive on these terms the 'complex' constituted by Ezra Pound and *The Cantos*—a 'complex' that is the concern of this book—is to do several things. We have begun—in this essay—by placing Pound's outward career, his set of immediately perceptible decisions not against a collection of newspaper headlines but against a long-range struggle. Thoreau said, 'Read not *The Times*, read the eternities.' We have to see Pound and *The Cantos* as being something more than 'newsworthy'. We have to see Pound and the poem on which he has laboured for a quarter of a century as part of the 'crisis' that has for half a century—or much, much more!—held Western civilization in a paralyzing grip. That is, we must resist taking up the lead, the cue, that Pound himself often gives us: that we are chiefly in the presence of an act of self-dedication, self-immolation. (We will not, of course, ignore the effects of this conviction on *The Cantos*.) We must resist, in this study of the poet as political animal, any sense that we are in the presence of a creature *sui generis*. We need not deny that *The Cantos* is indeed a poem whose political and esthetic aspects require all the powers of individual apprehension at our command; and it is, of course, these powers that must be put into play first. We need only reserve what Pound himself is unwilling to reserve: our assent to the proposition that Pound works uncompanioned at the task *The Cantos* represents. We should hope, instead, to see in the long run that, though Pound's poem is plainly the production of a man who has cobbled together special techniques for a special task, Pound himself cannot truly be said to be working alone.

The truth is that he is a member of a numerous company;

he shares (we shall see finally) not only a pervasive and quite conscious malaise about our culture (call it capitalist-democratic or something else). He shares, largely unconsciously, his conception of what the terms are on which a real resolution or relaxation of the malaise can be reached. He is not alone in his desire to 'make things new' (his recurrent phrase); he is not alone in his understanding of how the task may be carried to completion.

THE CANTOS
AS MEANS TO AN END

THERE are as many estimates of what Ezra Pound has accomplished in *The Cantos* as there are persons who put their minds—and, Pound would hope, their emotions—to comprehending the poem. The poem is a hoax (thus the reader hasty and insensitive); it is a pastiche of fine passages that deal with antique beauty and sections that bore incredibly when Pound turns to modern times with its banks and financial systems (thus the reader who is incurious as to the ideas that organize the pastiche); it is not a pastiche but a succession of calculated and violent juxtapositions effected in the interest of perfectly comprehensible ideas (thus the reader who troubles to see that Pound is no fool in prose and intends to be no fool in verse). Obviously, the line taken here is that Pound's long poem is neither hoax nor pastiche. It is a part—and to Pound the crucial part—of a life-long struggle to alter the world as it appears to Pound: a world in most areas hag-ridden by capitalist-democracy—more generally, by usury and its maleficent effects.

Comprehension of *The Cantos* involves—along with questions esthetic in import—recognition of this purpose and perception of how it shapes and directs the unrolling poem. In the later portions of the poem certain Chinese ideograms recur, inked symbols that (Pound tells) us epitomize what he believes, what he is trying to do in his poem. 'Make it new,' 'Call things by their right names' (this last is the Ching Ming ideogram so recurrent in the later sections of *The Cantos*), and the symbol for knowledge itself which contains, as its chief element, the mortar. (The first step toward really sound knowledge is to grind present knowledge—about which we are uncritical, which we take at face value—into a fine powder.) These frequent references to the intent of the entire poem suggest that love of obscurity *per se* has no place in Pound's programme for *The Cantos*. ('To communicate and then stop, that is the law of discourse,' writes Pound in Canto LXXX.) Rather, as we shall see, intelligibility must exist in combination with other elements in his programme—elements that exist because of the very limitations under which a modern poet labours—particularly when he writes in a language that has been 'captured' by a usurious civilization.

Therefore, the reader must, before he passes judgment on *The Cantos*, grasp what the aspirations of the poem are. Identification of these is aided by a reading of Pound's essays, but they can be traced in the poem itself; and they become more clear, more guiding, as the successive instalments of the poem become available. Hasty readers may report, with vexed tedium, that 'this time' Pound has 'worked up' Chinese history and John Adams or that—in *The Pisan Cantos*—there is a larger admixture of the autobiographical than is found in other sections. Careful readers are in a position to assess and understand the fluctuations. When they read Pound's essays, they have the pleasure of seeing their suspicions verified.

Furthermore, some misjudgments of *The Cantos* have roots outside the poem, in the common knowledge of what Pound's career has been. But such judgment as bases itself upon the facts of Pound's career arrives at a conclusion both irrelevant and untrue: *e.g.*, that in *The Cantos* the expatriate dabbler goes artistically as well as politically mad. This estimate ignores what Pound's essays and *The Cantos* permit one abundantly to see: that Pound's many departures (geographical and ideological) were not irresponsible departures, abnegations of responsibility. They were instructed, sharp-sighted protests, expressions of an exceptionally acute and inclusive sense of responsibility for Western culture. (In Pound, as I have said, we see the poet as political animal.) The various mistaken estimates are blind, do not see that Pound's economic views—in *The Cantos* as well as in his essay—are at many points similar to the political criticisms that home-abiding Americans levelled at their society during the war. Soberly (as we have shown) Pound's treason—his miscalculation—was to find in the programme of the Italian Fascist regime the promise of an economic and artistic reality that he had long sought. And his literary miscalculation (to many sympathetic readers of *The Cantos*) will remain his finding in his own programme for his poem the poetic analogue to what he found, politically, in the Fascist programme. For he judges that *The Cantos* is a work which will not only purify language; it will aid in the 'making new' of society itself.

One more misjudgment is one which bases itself on an acquaintance with Pound's early work and is apt to take the form of a question. Is it not likely that a man who gave his talents to translation and literary archeology would—when he tries to round out his career with a long work—end as Pound has ended in *The Cantos?*—with a farrago that displays once more a taste for the byways of poetry

27

and history? This query draws with it the suggestion that Pound's true poetic strength lay in the brief composition where absence of articulation was a minor flaw; it implies that Pound was unwise when he stopped translating from Rihaku, the Chinese poet whose brief excellence once enabled Pound to be briefly excellent in English verse.

II

This last set of objections represents a misconception about the entire body of Pound's poetry. It ignores—to embody here an observation Eliot passed concerning Pound's early poetry—the truth that translation can be for the poet as much a way of self-discovery as 'original' composition—that, indeed, translation which requires an adjustment of the poet's sensibility to that of his model may be more disciplinary and enlightening than a poem that purports to work directly from life. And it is not enough to say that without translation Pound would not have written his best early poetry. Without translation, Pound would not have written *The Cantos*.

'Without translation' here of course compends much more than the obvious sense of the phrase. Pound gives us a clue when he praises Gavin Douglas's translation of Vergil's Aeneid—a translation that, Pound judges, is superior to the Latin original because the Scot knew the sea and Vergil did not. To go farther, if Douglas had *not* translated Vergil, he would not have demonstrated (to himself, to us) that he *did* know the sea. Similarly, if Pound himself had not undergone the extensive discipline his various sorts of 'translation' afforded him, he would not be able to frame (for his own satisfaction, perhaps for ours) the protests *against*, the declarations *for*, which are woven

28

into *The Cantos*. Without his exploration, by whatever technical path was feasible, of various ages long past, Pound would not have met our own age, he would not have met himself, he would not have written *The Cantos*. He would not have placed in his poem his achieved understanding of the protests that sent him from America to Rapallo.

But a man does not build a house from planks that he has rejected. And Pound found his timber—with the partial exception of modern Italy—only by 'translation', by thought, by exploration of the possibilities that lie (in time) outside his own age. Thanks to this exploration—eclectic but not erratic—Pound arrived at a kind of stance outside what Léon Daudet called 'the stupid nineteenth century' and (for Pound) the equally stupid twentieth: a stance that it is well to sketch before we observe its power to organize *The Cantos*.

Mr. Pound once found heady amusement in a query of Eliot's: 'What does Mr. Pound believe?' Pound says the answer is quite simple: conformity to Confucius' *Ta Hio*, the path, the middle road. Before we accept this answer *tout court*, we should see of what elements it is composed. Pound's acceptance of the middle way crowns a series of contacts with persons and eras. Contact with the writings of the Sinologist Ernest Fenellosa (died 1908) was Pound's introduction to Eastern modes of artistic expression— one of the most telling of the many exposures and testings of Pound's own sensibility and taste. But it was thanks to the work of Fenellosa that Pound made the acquaintance of the Chinese ideogram: an acquaintance crucially important for *The Cantos*. But one must remain aware that other contacts—with Homer, with the poetry and civilization of Provence and Italy, with political aspects of Renaissance life, with certain of the American founding fathers—also 'tell' in a positive way for *The Cantos* and go to compose the list of loves that culminates in Pound's devotion to the *Ta Hio*.

Pound's hates also come from history, some of them. But it is natural that the majority of these should come from the present and the immediate past. Because of the laws of libel (and for cogent literary reasons) his hates are types (diplomats, munitions makers, liberal statesmen, and puritanical Americans) drawn from present-day life. Over the years, Pound's hatreds have become instructed ones—have been explained to him not merely by his contact with the relative excellence of other ages but by his acquaintance with certain modern economists who are critics of capitalist-democracy. Aided by these critics— some inside the democracies, some outside—Pound arrived at a dichotomy which pervades whatever he writes, which is the very backbone of *The Cantos*.

What does this guiding dichotomy come to? This. Modern life in capitalist countries is evil because it is pervaded by the spirit (*and* practice) of usury—usury, the taking of excessive interest on moneys lent, the enjoyment of rents that are no longer earned. A civilization dominated by banks and investment trusts loses all sense of what real value is (actual labour, actual property, commodities that can be actually enjoyed or consumed) and gives itself over to a vicious pursuit of values that are fictitious. The marks of this debasement can be seen not only in the classes that 'profit' by the social order; they are visible in the vulgarity of the multitude, whose tastes are so corroded that they can give no healthy response to the natural pleasures (the enjoyment of nature, the mysteries of love, birth, and even death) and can give no response whatever to the great art of the past or present. The multitude—and the multitude's betters—are capable only of an irritable pursuit of the new, the distracting, the machine-made artifact.

Consistent corollary of such a view—a criticism of England and America that has been expressed by many voices —is Pound's desire to use the pestle and mortar, to pound up old materials, somehow to make them new. What should the new thing be? This, Pound has found out by 'translation'. How is this new thing to be made? It is Pound's answer to this second question that is really idiosyncratic, that determines the form of *The Cantos*—a poem which is to be the means to the desired end, making our world new.

For reasons that will emerge in our discussion of the ideogram itself, Pound refuses to be specific about the pattern that the renewed society would have. But we can be sure that 'making new' means, negatively, the termination of usury and all usury draws with it. One of the worst of the consequences of usury, Pound argues, is a trust in abstractions or—more precisely—an abuse of abstractions, a use of them as a screen to hide from both the rulers and the ruled what is really 'up' in our civilization. Thus, 'liberty', 'progress', and 'free competition' conceal realities that Pound finds frightful. And so would we, did not a debased language cushion us against the shock of discovery. For the abstractions we keep repeating have no relation to what is really happening in the usurer's world; they serve, in that world, the function of deceptive ornament, non-functional and invalid. Thus, whoever seeks to make things new must guard against the blindness likely to afflict him as a member of our society. He must learn to distinguish between these concepts and what Pound calls

'ideas in ACTION' (Pound's capitals, which I drop).
'Ideas in action' never lapse into the inertness of general
statement; they must be perceived in specific contexts, for
they exist nowhere else. Pound quotes with admiration a
saying of Mussolini's; 'Why do you put your ideas in order?'
One supposes that to put one's ideas in order is to run the
risk of denaturing them, of putting up (though inadver-
tantly) still more screens in front of the sinister activity
of usurers. Pound calls himself a voluntarist; and a voluntarist, it is likely, has no savour of an idea until it exists in
a context of event, in a deed. (Lest we say glibly here,
'In short, a Fascist view,' let us observe that Pound at this
point is no more than anti-Aristotelian, one of a company
that includes many worthy men.)

One may say, then, of Pound's consciousness, enriched
by 'translation', that it fights against making a step that to
many minds is a natural one: abstraction from specific
instances. Pound's consciousness, instead, treasures the specific instances, resists temptations that make other men be
explicit about the relations perceived in a group of specific
instances. With Pound, it is otherwise. Only so long as
one sees certain men in certain poses, recalls certain striking
deeds, repeats certain notable lines, do the collective fruits
of 'translation' escape adulteration. Only 'ideas in action'
continue to ring changes that are vital; they do not fade
out into a chime heard only in the memory or—hideous
mishap!—a chime generalized. If our society is to be made
new, it must experience that stimulus that comes from
actually experienced ideas, 'ideas in action'; it must cease
to expect guidance from ideas which are abstracted from
reality, which are but the gibbering, impotent shades of
action.

It is just, I think, to say that Pound (in his essays and in

The Cantos) is guided by the undifferentiated aggregate of realized excellences, a vast and random collection of what an older theology would call 'the individuated good'. Shall we say that these excellences, these 'ideas in action', first made the appeal to the intuition or, better, stirred the will to mimicking what it beheld? Such an aggregate lacks specimens of ideas in the bad sense: a systematization of abstractions which no human being, Pound would say, has experienced and by which, consequently, all human beings are likely to be misled. 'Ideas in action' (volitions, desires, discriminations of taste) are good because they are felt to be good, not because they participate in *the* Good, an entity never directly experienced. The 'ideas in action' are good because they give us an immediate (and not a reasoned) sense that here a human possibility is fully realized. In short, Pound would have the human being treasure a set of vivid icons. A man should bedeck the halls of his memory with these because of their intrinsic vividness; and he should never ask, as he paces past them, 'Are they orthodox?' or 'Are they consistent with each other?' For a vivid experience is, one supposes, its own warranty; to ask whether it is compatible with other experiences is to fall into the sin of moralists who, at present, serve the usurers.

Despite this emphasis on the uniqueness of all excellence, Pound's thought does not steer entirely clear of 'system'. For, as a poet, Pound cannot work in direct, visual images; he cannot, like an actor, mimic actions. He is constrained to apply words to images and actions. Further, he happens (in his judgment) to use a language which bears the marks of usurious use, a language whose separate coins have been 'clipped'. Thus, renewal of civilization (by poetic means) involves reminting the language.

Many times Pound endorses the wisdom of the early Schoolman, Scotus Erigena, whose key-phrase, 'Authority is based on right reason,' catches Pound's fancy. (We have seen elsewhere that this Schoolman is the doctor—less than 'angelic', the Church says—who could lead Pound to Rome, if anyone could.) One might say that what Pound wishes to do is restate the sentence of Scotus Eriugena in voluntaristic terms. This restatement might be said to run thus: Authority—that is, the right to shape the perceptions of others, to control their actions—is based on sound and permanently cherished perceptions. Pound has no curiosity about deity; or, rather, sound perception records all we need to know of deity; it gives us 'deity in action'—deity realized, that is, in human action or in the purity of natural beauty. Pound's mockery, in *The Cantos*, of the Buddha's incarnation, his contempt for the waftiness of Taoist mysticism, his impatience with the rigid Hebrew God (and John Milton and the Jews)—all these gibes express Pound's feeling that God, if any, moves special persons to special acts. In perceiving these acts, we touch reality, touch God (if one wills)—touch God in the only way that can be useful in our work of reshaping.

III

Here—if in interdicted general terms—we have just stated the 'programme' of *The Cantos*. *The Cantos*, it is clear, cannot be regarded as a poem that exists for the glory of art. It is *im*pure poetry, calculated to deflect a stream of human events from a bad channel to a good one. Studying *The Cantos*, we can see how a poet (who is a political animal but may not make the direct attack possible to a political leader) defines and executes his assault.

One can commence with a series of negations. Pound will not employ the modes of conventional poetry; these modes are vitiated because of their association, in the popular mind, with glib fallacies about 'literature'— fallacies useful to the nineteenth century for setting apart, acknowledging, and then ignoring the poet—useful for dulling the impact of all verse. Further, romantic poetry (to which Pound considers his verse an antidote) becomes, with its yeasty imprecision, one of the chief aids to the vulgarizing of English. It blurs the precise meanings of words; it is intellectually uncritical, and it even lends itself to augmenting the prestige of ideas in *in*action, ideas which can threaten effectively no *status quo*. Therefore, from the vocabulary, from the techniques of popular romantic poetry (popular if any poetry is popular in 'Anglosaxon-dom') poetry must be diverted—if, that is, it is to be a source of renewal instead of a gratuitous prop to things as they are among the usurers and their vassals. But a precise redefinition of terms would be —notwithstanding Pound's respect for the Schoolmen—a second-best remedy. Best would be the invention and perfection of novel or startling techniques suited to 'tell' in this age, to 'tell' without ever flattering the grosser elements of this age.

In Pound's own eyes, his crucial innovation is the introduction of the Chinese ideogram into the writing of English poetry . . . verse that had become with the Georgians a series of obeisances to a herd of distrait white cows (theories of metre, diction, and proper subject as taught at American 'learneries'). To stress the importance of the ideogram for *The Cantos* is not to cancel Pound's debts to the troubadors or the French symbolists. But one may say that these other debts are incurred in order to consolidate the profit arising from the main one: the Chinese ideogram and its gift to a vitiated language and poetry.

In Chinese writing, the ideogram (Pound observes) is always a simplified picture of a *thing* (an object or a person) and recalls immediately the object or person or deed in question. Each ideogram, then, is tied to a real object— can never become detached from that object and (as in our culture) float off to be transformed, by distance and unfamiliarity, into an idea that tyrannizes over our minds. Recall here again Pound's fondness for the mortar which is the essential part of the Chinese ideogram for knowledge; so thought of, the process of coming to know something remains racy and familiar, does not become the august and perfectly empty process that (according to Pound) it usually is in Western culture.

Out of this fondness for the Chinese ideogram rises Pound's hope that, in *The Cantos*, he can renovate our poetry and the sensibility it arouses by discovering an English equivalent for the ideogram. He hopes that he can habituate his faithful reader to thinking in ideogram style and to so acting—can, that is, habituate the 'good' reader to thinking and acting in terms of concepts that have found expression in specific deeds at specific moments, concepts that have no existence apart from those specific deeds and moments. Only by following the clue of the ideogram will we be able to dispense with travel along the less desirable road of language renovation—that of precise redefinition of general terms in the spirit of the Schoolmen. So when Pound seeks to naturalize the spirit of the ideogram in English, he takes a path that is attractive to him for several reasons. The spirit of the ideogram—a suspicious phrase but the only one that offers at this point—does not permit ideas to exist as ideas in *in*action, *in vacuo*; it tends to force ideas to become or to remain 'ideas in action': ideas that we cannot know fully until, voluntaristically, we fall to imitating what a poem presents.

A supporting line of defence Pound returns to often is this one: we live in an age of science, and we should not ignore what makes possible the achievements of science; *au fond*, science triumphs because of an unconscious application of the method of the ideogram. For science, like the ideogram, is anti-Aristotelian and builds its hypotheses by observation and re-observation of what has taken place and is taking place. One has the sense—though Pound does not press the argument this far—that the laboratory sciences outstrip the social sciences because the social sciences are not yet fully detached from Aristotle, do not yet work (as do laboratory experimenters, as does Pound in *The Cantos*) in the spirit of the ideogram. Is it not in the backward social sciences that there persist the moribund abstractions that have no power to modify our evil society?

This is, in brief, Pound's plea for domesticating the ideogram (or, more accurately, a poetic method obedient to its spirit) in our culture. That culture—always weak because of the mode in which ideas tend to exist there—will take over, from the ideogram, a strength, a sort of sensing and acting ignored entirely by us for many centuries; if we ever draw near to it, we do unconsciously, by gross chance. Even the Curies, Pound would argue, do not see the social and artistic equivalents of what they do in the laboratories. Only a few minds—one of these, of course, is Pound's—have seen how the scientific spirit, the spirit of the ideogram, can become operative in other contexts than that of science itself.

IV

Pound, in *The Cantos*, is concerned with these other contexts: the social and artistic equivalents of the scientific method. He wishes to explore—in terms of *his* vocabulary now—the power of the ideogram to vivify verse and reorient society. Much in *The Cantos* (not all) that perplexes the reader about Pound's choice of subject-matter and his way of presenting it becomes intelligible if we perceive that the spirit of the ideogram is at work, shaping and selecting.[1] At any rate, the poem works out (or often does) an equivalent in English to what (supposedly) is accomplished by the actual Chinese symbol. Yet any reader who approached *The Cantos* with my previous remarks and his own recollections of Pound's renderings of the Chinese poets in mind would be (save for very brief and isolated passages) bewildered. Chinese poetry (as we sense its nature through the translations of Pound and others) exploits the essence of the ideogram (its lichen-like adherence to a tiny area of bed-rock reality) by associating particular objects (the late moon, a flight of stairs, a woman waiting) that have not been put together before—objects that, juxtaposed in their unaltered simplicity, create (in the reader's or hearer's mind) a totality of apprehension that takes in far more than what, in the poem, is stated. So understood, composition in Chinese reminds one of the creation of patterns made possible by a turn of the child's toy, the kaleidoscope. The toy itself creates as well as the movement of the child's hand; in Chinese (one

---

[1] For *The Cantos* to be specifically intelligible at all points, grasp of the general method is *not* enough. One must equal or work toward the linguistic range, the varieties of literary and historical information that Pound feels is relevant to his problem: namely, the identification of our age for what it is, an age of usury, and its termination.

senses) the language itself as well as the poet. I force the analogy to this extreme point only to prepare for my assertion that in *The Cantos* Pound is striving for an equivalent of the effect of Chinese poetry, not (as in his earlier translations from Rihaku) a reproduction of the effect. English, after all, has its limiting grammar structure; it is the product of a complex and even tainted history. As I have said, the ideogram gave the clue for the method of *The Cantos*; but *The Cantos* resembles no Chinese poem that (by the kindness of Legge, Lowell, Tietjens, Waley, and others) has come to our notice.

Strict imitation of the Chinese method was what Pound once practised; and the results he allied to those of the imagist movement. Pound's own later judgment on that movement (which strove to render the object in terms of itself) casts direct light on the observed difference between *The Cantos* and the translations from the Chinese. The 'programme' of the imagist movement was not wrong, but it was incomplete. It led to the production of static poetry, poetry devoted only to objects and what could be their precipitate when introduced into the minds of readers. Imagism was incapable of presenting, of 'rendering', things which were dynamic rather than static. This is the observation that leads us directly to *The Cantos*; for we have seen that it is a poem that has, as its *raison d'être*, the creation of a change in our culture by directing our attention to that which is always changing, culture itself. It exists to present—in the phrase which Pound has given us—'ideas in action'. To realize this ambition takes Pound beyond the limited interests of Chinese poetry (as we know it), and also beyond what seem the similar and also limited interests of imagism. Since in *The Cantos* Pound is playing for a great stake—the alteration of the cluster of customs by which we live (*Paideuma* is Pound's word for such a cluster)—what Pound needs is the effect of directness the ideogram permits without, however, restriction of its use to the areas of lyric sensibility, of nuance, where (apparently) it has its triumphs in Chinese.

Pound sees to it that his poem comprehends a much larger area, the region taken up by a motley multitude of 'ideas in action'. Shall we say that each 'idea in action' is the equivalent of the single Chinese ideogram, and that all the 'ideas in action' combine (just as do the ideograms) to suggest, in the mind of the reader, a totality of thought, of comment, greater than that which is explicitly advanced in the poem? At any rate, the range of *The Cantos* is as wide (if not as thorough) as that of a great culture-history like A. J. Toynbee's *A Study of History*. Pound would contend that, thanks to the method just indicated, his poem is superior to any orderly, systematized culture-history in several respects. The culture-historian addresses his account chiefly to our powers of comprehension, giving those 'faculties' the keen but—Pound would say— unfruitful pleasure of seeing how the historical panorama has gone together. History is more—Pound's poem suggests—than a succession of perfectly intelligible *faits accomplis*. And from such studies as Toynbee's are absent —have suffused—the bouquet of a deed and the quiddity of a person; all that remains is an abstract judgment or so. History is not something to be systematized or put in order. (Again one recalls Mussolini's 'Why do you put your ideas in order?') History must be 'intuited', must be experienced by the will as well as by the intelligence. Only by being impelled to mimic an action can one learn what an 'idea in action' once was or might again be. One must be *involved* with Malatesta, John Adams, Cavalcanti,

Jefferson. It is useless to dally with them, as we do when we read conventional history. We must 'translate' them if the gifts of past experience are to flower at all in our lives. Such a 'translation' *The Cantos* will enable us to make.

The superiority, then, of *The Cantos* to what covers much the same ground, culture-history, is (Pound points out) his poem's compression, its immediacy, its effects of coercion which force the reader to 'intuit' rather than comprehend. Orderly narrative, study of causal relation-ships, precise statement of the basis for comparisons made —all this is an invitation to comprehend or (the same thing) to escape the urgency of the real experience which puts (and should put, Pound feels) the will in chancery; for the mind is encouraged to catalogue and file for delayed reference the very 'ideas in action' that ought to be seminal. But another method of presentation—naturally, the method of *The Cantos*—will compel the reader to an act of direct experiencing, confused (why not?) and intense. And only from the latter sort of reading—the argument must run— do conviction and action come.

What does the reader find in *The Cantos* if he insists on trying to comprehend as well as 'intuit'? First, he is sure that intuition is indeed given free play—more, he feels at the outset, than it is capable of profiting from; for the voyages of Odysseus, religious processions, immolated youths, and Renaissance condottiere beat on it a demanding tattoo. In contrast to this, the reader may note that there are indeed sections in which attention is fixed on one person or one topic. But even here intuition (or the will) is assaulted by a wide variation of styles for various subject-matters: the rolling rhythms for Odysseus and the sea, the broken yet savage movement of verse for the hell of usurers, the almost elegiac accents that lament a world riddled by usury, the compressed and not entirely intelligible prosiness that Pound has drawn from the decrees of popes and doges, from the letters of Jefferson and John Adams. Nor within these rhythmical units is there much comfort for what we might call the easy reader; for many a plain effect of rhythm or thought is overlaid by variations in pace, by interventions of auctoral comment, by descent to bombast, by interposition of slang—effects that all (in one way or another) 'guy' a tone just established. The easy reader, then, will conclude that those who say the poem is dadaist or a hoax or (more generously) a tessellation of the exquisite and the hideously flat are near the truth. Not so. Such a reader may indeed describe his own reactions adequately; but he has fallen short of what the poem, by its very method, demands of him. He displays— to put the case *for* the poem as strongly as one may—the flaccid, dispersed attention which is all that the literature of the age of usury demands of him. He has not risen to an opportunity. The deplorable habits of our culture are too strong for him; the spirit of the ideogram, as realized in *The Cantos*, has been defeated, put to nought.

The more sturdy reader might have recourse to two books by Pound—books which describe, in another context, the methods of *The Cantos* (*The ABC of Reading*) or display the methods within prose limits (*Culture*). Particularly illuminating for *The Cantos* is Pound's procedure in *The ABC of Reading*. Here Pound, in a book designed to form the taste of Anglo-Saxon readers (and how the book is, in Pound's view, needed!), gives a few guiding remarks and then puts the reader into relation with passage upon passage of poetry. The reader will learn what good poetry is, Pound insists, not by idle chatter about abstract standards but by contact with poetry—*language* in action, one might say—by a succession of sensations. Pound calls this paideutic scientific in technique; he also sees it as education under the beneficent sign of the ideogram. For out of the initial confusion of reading will emerge the only real certainty that a student can have as to what good poetry is. But that certainty can never be anything more than an aggregate of experiences of reading poetry—in our term, 'intuiting' poetry. It does no good to reason about poetry, to think about what in general it does, what it ought to be. Likewise, the other volume, *Culture*, a disorderly book, is an exposure of the reader to many experiences of culture-patterns within the narrowest possible limits; it is as if one should not speculate about culture-patterns and changes but have violent contact with *cultures* in action. Both books share the thesis, then, that it is only by direct exposure that the will can be stirred to changes in taste, to deviations of desire.

Similarly, only by a poem like *The Cantos*, the counter-part in verse of the works we have just noted, can the stream of individual sensibility, of collective action, be diverted from an old channel to a new one. Construction engineers are not sensitive about the ugly scars their machines make on a terrain; their intent is fixed on the requisite task. Pound, one gathers, is indifferent to the damage his machine, *The Cantos*, works on present linguistic conventions and culture-patterns. The end—a reconstituted society—will justify the damage involved in transition.

So viewed, *The Cantos* take on—not order, for that is not what is desired—but the clear appearance of being a calculated assault on indurated modern sensibility: sensibility that an orderly attack (cultural histories, analyses of Western thought) leaves unaltered. And how does one decide what that sensibility ought to give up, ought to turn to? Certainly not by reasoning from general principles offered us (say) by Aristotle and Aquinas. One comes to a valid answer (inside the limits of the poem, and without) by being exposed to as many 'cultures in action' as can be wedged into the poem. At least, this is precisely what (for the successful reader) is accomplished in *The Cantos*. Each culture-fragment is a hard block, a fact that cannot dissolve in poetic fancy. The block associated with similar blocks gives rise to an inclusive impression that over-arches the component parts of the poem—that, indeed, over-arches much more. Yet this lasting impression owes its rightness to the method that provoked it. We are told that there are no grammatical links in Chinese; be that as it may, there are certainly no *logical* links in *The Cantos*, and it remains with each reader to create for the poem a more or less intelligible rationale.

He will create this so far as his intuition and (*I* say) intelligence permit—the over-arching of meaning, of sensed comment, both complex analogues to the very simple arch that the Chinese hearer builds for some brief collocation of ideograms. But one must not forget that the arch one builds for *The Cantos* is not simple; for each reader must put together an empyrean, a crystal sphere that will majestically span the entirety of the poem. The sphere thus constituted must light up the entire work—but without becoming a system, without losing touch with each 'idea in action' that is supposed to have the validity, the unshakable claim to being real that each ideogram has in a brief Chinese poem. And, though the sphere over-arches, it must at the same time touch every single point that it hangs above.

To alter the figure, to state the case *for* the method as

44

strongly as I am able: the method of the poem serves as a midwife to ideas, and serves better than Socrates ever did because, from Pound's point of view, all of Socrates's ideas (abstractions that they were) came into the world still-born. Because of the orienting of Socrates' own mind, each idea was deprived of breath, became a non-entity. But the ideas given being by *The Cantos* remain 'ideas in action', with a breath and passion that permit them to move our wills as well as our understanding. Further, any other arrangement of the poem (a more lucid one, for example) would deprive the work of its claim on us, its power over us. So, at any rate, I read Pound's hope.

Viewing the poem thus, aided by an acquaintance with Pound's prose utterance, the reader should be able to read *The Cantos* with an enlightened as well as an assaulted intuition. The enlightenment soon takes this form: all civilizations fall into two groups—those tainted with usury and those free from it. The civilization that is free of interest-slavery, rent-subjugation, and credit inflation has a *chance* to be human; whereas the society that is not thus free has very little chance of attaining distinction.

How all this is specifically conveyed, the means employed by Pound for the creation of *his* extension of the ideograms his variations in diction, the apparently calculated effects, that arise from the juxtaposition of the blocks of the poem, the suggestions (even) of a kind of progress or arrangement throughout the poem—perception of this will sharpen one's view of the work, but it will not alter the outlines sketched here.

Further, were the purpose of the analysis in this section estimation and not (what is needed for *The Cantos* in the first place) comprehension, other questions would require answer. Later, we must look at the key-concept of 'ideas in action' and ask whether it is truly the neck-verse for older ways of thinking. We must ask whether the dichotomy of civilizations into usurious and non-usurious is as fruitful a one as Pound thinks it is. But these questions can wait. What calls for present recognition is this: the kind of ambition that has produced *The Cantos*. It seems to me an utterly sincere one. Further, the choice of method for its realization is (within the limits rigidly drawn by Pound's guiding ideas and his sensibility) quite defensible, or at least is not a product of a desire to mystify. It is, rather, an expression of Pound's wish to edify. Or, one may say, taking into view Pound's entire programme, to re-edify.

THE DEVICES
OF POUND'S CANTOS

THE devices of Inigo Jones are familiar to us, through historical description and also in the poetry which anticipated them (*e.g.*, Spenser's) or was produced concurrently. A court masque was an elaborate theatrical representation abounding in a mixture of poetry *per se*, dramatic action, unlocalized declamation, the dance—to all of which variety were superadded the effects made possible by 'machines': the flight of Icarus, waterfalls, and horrendous explosions from Erebus. All this constituted a representation from which the viewer drew, we suppose, a large number of disparate pleasures—pleasures that might or might not combine into one pleasure: say, the perception that Eliza or James had been glorified, that a certain virtue had triumphed over a certain vice. Likewise, to many a reader, the poetry of Spenser (serious and exalted in the ethics it attached itself to) seems also a masque: a succession of devices that dazzle in themselves but that do not effectively support the intended allegory, that are (indeed) likely to support *several* allegories. (Does not Emile Legouis apply the term *tapestry* to *The Faerie Queene* to indicate the predominance of diversion and decoration over conformity to a basic design?) At any rate, the masque and poems like Spenser's, whatever our

47

final measure of them, demand a mode of apprehension that we do not now readily provide—that, indeed, many readers (discouraged by what seems to them irrelevant, or merely ingenious and precious—antiquarian in a bad sense) do not think it worth while to provide. For such readers—to be Chestertonian—the masque remains a series of masks: emblems or devices scarcely worth the labour of grasping.

A like feeling may associate itself with the reading of Ezra Pound's *Cantos*. Here again the disparate elements are—if our knowledge of history and language is equal to the task Pound sets—intelligible. But satisfactory reading of the poem requires us to cope, further, with a succession of devices—the spurts of Greek fire, the mountain that opens to disclose a richly hung grotto—that Pound has provided. Some readers, then, relinquish *The Cantos* in somewhat the spirit they give up Spenser's poem. The devices, of course, are not parallel; but the discouragement they produce is. The labour of mastering the 'drift' that the devices are associated with seems too costly of attention and patience. And against such an ebbing of curiosity there is no further argument. But there remain (for Pound as for Spenser) readers who feel that it is wrong to assume that a complex poem is the product either of perverse ingenuity or of intellectual pride—readers who, further, feel that out of a scrutiny of the devices, the 'machines' which a poet displays, is likely to emerge meaning. This feeling has 'paid off' (if variously) for Spencer; it can also 'pay off' for Pound and *The Cantos*, and in terms which the rhetoric and the devices of the poem itself provide. (Just as it is false to suppose that James's courtiers found delight only in the bombards that Inigo Jones ordered set off, it is unwise to conclude that Pound's sympathetic readers can go no further than feeling delight only in the obvious bravura passages of the poem.) Therefore, the methods of reading that I am going to identify are, I think, in accord with Pound's inclusive purpose in *The Cantos* and his conception of the proper way to gratify that purpose. (*The Cantos*, recall, are an attack on the usurer's civilization in which we live; they also draw our attention to the comparative excellence of civilizations which escaped usury and achieved—well, not heaven, but humanity.)

The rhetoric of *The Cantos* consists of Pound's striking out in a variety of directions—directions not logically consistent with each other. But it is not on the basis of logic that Pound would have the effectiveness of his rhetoric judged. He is concerned with coercing the emotions to follow a new and proper course, with altering the volition of his readers. The will, it is true, may be taken by frontal attack (and a good deal of Pound's rhetoric *is* frontal attack); but if it seems likely that sorties from other directions will cause the citadel to capitulate, no good tactician will demur because the projected sorties might mar the supposed 'purity' of an all-over plan. We shall—to use an earlier figure—observe a multitude of masks and devices of a rhetorical order that Pound holds up between us and him —holds up with a malice that we may too hastily misread as wilfulness. Perhaps we would be more likely to estimate some of them justly, these dodges and sleights always purposeful, if we discovered their beginnings in Pound's earlier work.

Here, I think, there are two habits of composition that are useful to isolate: one, the habit of imagism (closely related to the ideogram of Chinese poetry); and, two, the habit of the dramatic monologue. Both of these habits provide Pound—in his early poetry and, curiously, in *The*

Cantos, a poem with a 'programme'—with a technique of disavowal, of withdrawal from the onus of responsibility for what has been said. That Pound—in pre-*Canto* days—should have desired effects of disavowal is understandable, is but part of his general protest against romantic poetry, in which so often is traceable the poet's *personal* embrace of all that experience presents him. Too often the romantic poet keeps reminding us that he *is* embracing all experience, and that the experience embraced is, first and foremost, *his* experience. Thus, any sort of reality—the reality that Pound has faith in, persons and places that existed or exist at a certain time—is, in romantic poetry, perceived only mistily through a cloud that the poet's enthusiasm suffuses over concrete objects, distorting and even hopelessly disguising that which was, in the first place, 'given'. Pound's early styles, then, seem to aim at correcting romantic excesses—are designed to cut back the rank, needless growth in the garden of poetry, to establish (for the person who walks there) the outlines of the objects themselves, to assert the integrity adhering in the object presented. So viewed, a poem is chiefly successful in its power to suggest the qualities, the nuances, of the object—qualities and nuances that are felt to exist independent of whatever the poet may feel about the object that he is presenting.

As I have said, two techniques were of notable service to Pound as he went about his task of rectifying outlines and restoring nuances—techniques that minimize if they do not cancel out the personality of the poet. These are the techniques of imagism and of the dramatic monologue.

Imagism—its practitioners tell us—was an effort to return to the object, to render it in its own terms, rather

than peer at it myopically through the mist that rises, on
the slightest encouragement, from the poet's own yeasty
soul. Or if the object cannot be rendered in its own terms
(what object can be since the practice of any art implies
selection and limitation of means?), it should be—in poetry
—rendered in as close an approximation to those terms
as language can provide. Later—it is true—Pound censured imagism as it was practised; he censured it because
it came to regard as its proper subject the inert natural
phenomenon: the fir tree, the wave. Its practicers did not
grow in grace, did not perceive that they must not rest
satisfied with rendering the natural object, must further
develop means (as non-romantic, as lucid and astringent)
of presenting the human, the non-static. (This contrast
between static natural objects and dynamic human ones
is practically all Pound has in mind when he uses, in his
criticism, the phrase 'ideas in action'; there are no Platonic
overtones, no suggestion that 'ideas' 'realize' themselves
in human action. Ideas, for Pound, exist only in separate
human actions and are not to be detached from them.
The poet—whether 'classic' or 'romantic'—takes the
wrong track when he tries to learn or invent techniques
for the 'rendering' of ideas or concepts; for he proceeds
to concern himself with that which is both non-existent
and pernicious. The poet—any poet—cannot, however,
take his ease in the world of nature, serving the five senses
in their intense purity; he must learn to do justice to that
which escapes the five senses in their purity—the human,
the 'idea in action'.) One may anticipate and suggest that
the other 'devices' novel in *The Cantos* serve to make more
flexible and responsive to the wider task the earlier techniques of imagism: to preserve, that is, their basic excellence,
the tone of disavowal, and to overcome their defect: their

tendency to static treatment of a limited subject-matter.

One should note also—before turning to the dramatic monologue and its value as a technique of disavowal— that Pound's early efforts to render the object had of course sanction from another quarter: the example of Chinese poetry as Pound, in the studies of Ernest Fenellosa, came to know it. The connection, for Pound, between imagism and Chinese poetry is easy to state. One may put the matter thus: imagism comes easily to the Chinese, whereas it is difficult for us of the West; for our intellectual history is (in Pound's opinion) disfigured by the recurrence of useless abstractions, and our poetry is given up to suffusions of overt, misty egotism. With the Chinese—fortunate mortals!—the basic unit of written expression is the ideogram: a symbol for a word in which persists, for the instructed, a picture of the object the word referred to at the very outset of its history. The Chinese poet, then, is fortunately bound to objects; his poetry can be no more than a tasteful arrangement of them which will coerce comment in the mind of his hearer or reader—comment that the poet is not allowed (by the canons of his art as well as by the nature of his language) to make himself. In contrast, the Western poet must, by a great effort of will and intelligence, put aside the evil habits natural to Western expression: the facility of composition made possible by the abundance of abstractions, the coincident habit of exploiting the ego rather than the thing to be 'rendered'. Indeed, it is consciously that the Western poet must bind himself to objects; and no matter how firm he makes the bonds, he will continue to work with the uneasy sense that knots are slipping, permitting him (if he is unwary) to fall back on abstractions or into the vagaries of personal emotion. (Pope and Swinburne illustrate, for

Pound, these two perils. Pound prefers the Pope-alternative; the effect of over-precision is better than the love of imprecision which is all that romantic egotism comes to, in poetry.)

The other support, in the early Pound, to the mode of disavowal was the dramatic monologue. A form of long lineage ending in the poetry of Browning (whom Pound respects), it provides the form in which much of the early poetry and *The Cantos* as well are set. And one can say that Pound at this point differs from Landor—the last civilized Englishman, in Pound's opinion—in that all Landor's *Imaginary Conversations* are washed over with the clear lacquer of Landor's elegant, removed attitude; whereas Pound strives, in expression, for the maximum of idiosyncrasy, this to correspond, to be sure, to the idiosyncrasy of the speaker being presented. And one can say—with still greater profit, if we wish to make clear the process of disavowal by means of the dramatic monologue—that Pound's use of the form differs from Browning's in several ways. For Browning, in turn, can be distinguished from Landor thus: Landor's clear wash of transparent lacquer creates a high degree of regularity and polish; Browning's unclear wash creates a surface tinted and crazed with the hue and cleavages that adhere to Robert Browning and to the subject he has chosen (by this I mean the word-order, the violent transitions of thought, the compression of diction). And this 'wash' of Browning's (readers will testify) goes deeper—penetrates to the very core of ideas and attitudes that (supposedly) are simply the property of Dr. Sludge the Medium. It so penetrates that all of Browning's 'personae', however local and odd they are to our first view, *tend* to become Robert Browning himself, not only in diction but in the central insight that is finally

53

teased out. The process is so complete in *Rabbi ben Ezra*
(who tries to think of him as a figure at all?) that hasty
readers are likely, say, to miss the more subtle approximations in Dr. Sludge. Yet approximations are there—there
and elsewhere. They exist probably because of Browning's
own imperious sense that a basic collection of truth exists
towards which every human being, given his head, will
grope and stumble. Sometimes the chosen character stops
far short of these truths; but a great many of the characters
Robert Browning treats display, at any rate, the stigmata
of the orientation that the poet sensed in himself.

So for Browning the dramatic monologue was not a
means of disavowal (nor was it, I think, for Landor).
It was, instead, the means of the strongest possible sort
of avowal: one that outpaced the conventional romantic
poet who suffuses a given experience with his beliefs and
hopes. Browning's egotism was more imperious; it asserted
that his view was not merely his own but the view that
humanity (whoever the chosen specimen) inclines toward.

What was with Browning—and perhaps Landor—a
vehicle for pronounced avowals was, from an early date,
a means of disavowal for Pound. Pound, I feel, does not
know his historical periods better than Browning his;
but he treats them better—not translating them (somehow,
anyhow) into terms in instructed and optimistic panthe-
istic argument, but preserving them in an aura proper to
their own times, keeping them close-related to their own
'paideuma'. ('Paideuma' is a recurrent word in Pound's
prose; he borrows it from the anthropologist Frobenius
who uses it to designate the collection, the 'configuration',
of habits that mark a person and attach him to a culture
from which he cannot—without gross injustice—be separ-
ated.) In terms of the present analysis, Browning's 'sin' is

covertly to place his personages in comparatively specious conjunction to the 'paideuma' of the poet's own time or the poet's own belief. A contrasting task is Pound's in *The Cantos*: that of effecting a conjunction between chosen historical personages and Pound's own 'paideuma' without, however, doing violence to the 'paideuma' proper to each historical personage. But, in doing all this, Pound remains faithful to his earlier tone of disavowal, in the dramatic monologue and elsewhere. Hence, some of the trouble of *The Cantos*, since what strikes us at first is the effectiveness of the disavowal; yet all specific disavowals are, at last, to be related to some aspect of Pound's own views, his 'paideuma'—are there because of his views.

All this extended comparison of Browning and Pound is not made with the intent of censuring Browning for what he has done; it is to establish clearly how Pound's approach to a Chinese frontier guard is different from Browning's to Sludge the Medium. It is not to be facetious to say that Pound wishes (in imagist terminology) to 'render' the guard, the 'idea in action'; whereas Browning wishes to display the Browning that moves—imperfectly, unrealized —in Sludge the Medium.

Both devices—imagism and the dramatic monologue— served in earlier days to insulate Pound from the sin and danger of overt personal utterance. Safe in this insulation he might (as have some other modern poets) have continued to operate: within the limits of concrete objects, within the confines of carefully explored historical personalities. It is, in fact, T. S. Eliot's opinion that the early Pound does better with personalities that have their locus in distant history than with the factitious modern figures which Pound —perhaps to avoid libel suits, more likely to avoid the depressing effects of the journalistic—must hammer together.

Why then, did the earlier Pound, scrupulous artist in disavowal, approach material that was dangerous—'dangerous' in that it threatened and sometimes quite plainly destroyed that mood of dispassion which, when one treats historical subjects, it is easy to sustain? Why not, that is, remain content with extremely shrewd and delicate 'translation'—content with occupations that do not stir one, that do not enlist one in support of a cause?

Pound came to approach the 'dangerous'—and *The Cantos* is, in this connection, an unceasing dwelling among what is dangerous to the artist in detachment—because of his very triumphs in the realms of detachment. Was it that, after for so long feeling and rendering so well distant ages and persons, he could not resist, in *The Cantos*, doing full, rounded justice to an age he loathed responding to, the present age? True, a manifest and augmenting cause of Pound's hatred of our century—a hatred that is the 'go' of *The Cantos*—is the continued general indifference to Pound's poetry and learned studies. But this personal irritation is supplemented by a general view of our century: a view which, I think, is not invalidated by its association with Pound's personal frustration. In short, because Pound has come to know the excellence of other ages—by his studies, by his direct translations, by his 'translations' that take the form of dramatic monologue—he is constrained to repudiate an age which, he judges, is hopelessly stained by capitalistic democracy.

The motive force, then, of much of his earlier poetry is the poet's dispassionate disavowal of his own preoccupations. He has had enough (as reader as well as writer of poetry) of what Mario Praz called 'the romantic agony'.

He sees, in the writing of poetry, the poet's chance to sub-limate his own preoccupations (if he cannot cancel them): a sublimation that consists of—we have seen—the 'correct' presentation of a physical object, an historical person. In contrast to this, the motive force behind *The Cantos* (which continue to employ the devices that we have already noted, which employ complex extensions of these devices) is the passionate avowal of the poet's hatred of the present usurious age—an avowal made in behalf of the same ego which Pound wished to rule out as motive force in his earlier poetry. I do not here wish, by insisting on this contrast, to imply that Pound's pre-1920 poetry was anti-romantic and that *The Cantos* (the vehicle of his hatred) are romantic. It is more precise, more accurate, to say that Pound has become passionate in the name of dispassion. He wishes to show why, in our culture, disavowal (an admirable, esthetically profitable attitude) is—like other humane attitudes—now difficult if not impossible. Yet he would seem to wish to continue to employ the techniques proper to disavowal in a work that is intended to avow, to assert.

From this central circumstance (the sustaining in a long, complex poem of a surface appearance of not committing oneself) arise the confusions, the sense of devices employed without a sufficient rationale, all that makes *The Cantos*, for some readers, a vexing raree-show. Yet the poem is passionately intended: readers must be made to see that the corrosion of our civilization by usury is nowhere a peripheral issue. But the means that most readers might think proper for expression of passionate avowal—explicit general statement, uncomplex narrative, and so forth—have been stolen and debased by nineteenth century literature. So Pound still pins his faith on the efficacy of devices that avoid the facile assertion and presentation characteristic of the literature he detests. By continuing to renounce these, he assures for *The Cantos* the alert attention that Chinese poetry wins from its hearers, that all sorts of disavowal assure; the poet's sincerity is proved by his so clearly having nothing at stake. We have been wooed so often passionately by poetry that a dispassionate, disavowing courtship is the only one that is likely, in this age, to win our agreement.

So the modes of the earlier poetry are continued and complicated in *The Cantos*. Modes meant for one function (disavowal) serve in another: passionate avowal or passionate repudiation, as you will. A metaphor may serve to stress this distinction. I have suggested that, in Pound's early poetry, the mask, the 'persona' in the old sense, was welcome because it entirely concealed the poet's face, his own being. Now, in *The Cantos*, which continue to employ the mask, which are (in large part) a succession of masks, the successful emergence of glints of Pound's own malice are of the essence of his effort. The glints must shine through the eye-slits of the various masks; they are glints that the reader must perceive—and, so perceiving, perceive what the devices are used for, what central attitude they come from. Further, the contrived succession of the masks must make an assertion that Pound is loath to make: the assertion, however, that is the be-all and end-all of *The Cantos*.

To be specific, what are the precise changes in the techniques already recognized and now to be traced in *The Cantos*? First, there continues, in impersonal presentations of objects of nature and certain civilizations, the mode of early imagism: a mode suited in Pound's judgment only to the 'rendering' of static objects. Second, there is what one may call a broadened imagism, to take in what Pound terms 'ideas in action': these the total of human reality, innocent of abstractions. For this second kind of passage, 'declamation' is a convenient and just identifying term; it has nothing to do with the continuations of the dramatic monologue which can be observed in *The Cantos*.

Third, one must observe that the Chinese ideogram no longer inspires simply the rendering of specific objects. It has become the key to the organization of the entire poem. Recall that the Chinese poet coerces, within the limits of a brief poem, an all-over reaction by a selection and association of concrete objects, the Chinese word-symbols. Why may an English-writing poet not perform an act of coercion also: analogous but not the same, on a greater scale, in a language whose tyrannies will remain quite unlike the beneficent ones of the Chinese? By a selection and association of concrete objects (chiefly persons or 'ideas in action') all without direct comment, the poet should be able to force the reader to perform a task much more complex, it is true, than that which the reader of Rihaku performs—more complex but in a way the same: the over-arching meaning will be the reader's creation, not (in an explicit sense, at least) the poet's.

Fourth, a specific and recognizable variety of this method, the masks, the personae: these, when employed, must— by choice, by association, even by presentation—allow the glints of Pound's own malice or admiration to reach us.

Are there additional devices? I shall discuss two others: a peculiar use of pronouns *outside* the mask-sections, often in the sections of declamation (the sections, that is, that render 'ideas in action' rather than static material objects); the employment of what Pound calls logopoeia (by defini-tion, the tricks that are peculiarly available to the artist who works in the medium of language—in this instance, the English language).

What, more generally, I hope to show by the following analysis is that Pound's development of the devices of disavowal and his invention (in a relative sense) of several others become a rhetoric of passionate avowal and repudiation, both animated by Pound's harsh, dichotomous perception of the history of culture: richness of civilization in ages free of usury; brutalization and decay of human powers in an age of usury. In other words, as for Spenser, so for Pound. The parade of a selection of devices becomes intelligible once the rationale for them is provided. In Spenser, the key to the allegory, abundant and interlocking. In Pound, the reason for employing certain methods of presentation. The existence—and even the nature—of this reason, the reader of *The Cantos* themselves ought to suspect (just as the reader of Spenser ferrets out a good many meanings unaided). I do not, however, pretend that the following explanation of poetic method is drawn entirely from *The Cantos* or could be. Indeed, it has already drawn upon Pound's earlier poetic practice and it follows up additional clues that exist in Pound's prose criticism. Thus, to the taste of some readers, my approach is one that violates 'the integrity of the poem'; I hope, however, it enables me to show to others that the integrity is there.

II

The direct legacy of earlier imagism readers will feel and recognize chiefly in the sections which present nature uncorrupted and health-giving. The descriptions of the landscapes and halls through which Ulysses and his fellows pass, the *pictures* from Chinese history, the religious and secular processions from Renaissance history—all these and similar sections are, as I conceive the matter, in the mode of imagism and that of the closely related ideogram (that is, the ideogram *un*developed in the classification I have made). Without exception, their appearance in the poem, detached and elegiac, is an indication that the following counter is being advanced by Pound: here, in the poem, emerges a section of experience that is unspoiled, that is undamaged by the taint we find in modern culture; here is the sort of experience that is non-moral but good because within the limits proper to it Pound's apprehension is able to operate without the supervenience of the anger that finds expression, in *The Cantos*, either in the direct fury of the hell sections or in those that concern makers of munitions; or (less directly) in the mask-sections in which the guise of the American tourist, say, does not keep us from perceiving the glint in the eye-slits. (*E.g.*, Cantos XIV, XV, XVIII, XXVIII.) Further, one should note that, in the sections that have to do with early man, the subject can still be rendered in the mode imagistic (nature, which is never for Pound in any sense dynamic; human nature in so far as it is in stasis and is not to be sharply distinguished from nature), neither the mask nor still more difficult devices are employed. Indeed, in these passages, the earlier mood of disavowal is employed with perfect fitness because, paradoxically, there is nothing to disavow; there is nothing to disturb the poise of the calm, impersonal report on the sea, on Ulysses passing over the sea. Nor should the circumstance that this device is quite lucid, is clear glass held up before the object, leave us in any confusion about Pound's attachment to any object thus presented. He is able to do it this honour because there is in it no admixture of dishonour; the clear glass is sufficient. Those who regard *The Cantos* as pastiche will say, perhaps grudgingly, of these sections (*e.g.*, Cantos I, II, and LXXX) that in such places the object presented is quite attractive, the movement of the verse steady and distinguished. Yet we, as careful readers, should do more than enjoy these passages in themselves. We should see these sections as a contribution to the cumulative meaning of the poem: bright *loci* placed in the poem to coerce in us the perception of what darkness *is* darkness; fresh regions from which rises the almost odourless aroma that trains our nostrils to sense putridity.

But, as Pound has indicated, the limitation of imagism (even thus extended) is that it does not allow the poet to present 'ideas in action'; imagism suffices for the still poise of nature, but it is unequal to rendering man as man: man when he ceases to be a part of nature (as, in Pound's treatment, Ulysses is)—man when he is truly man and dissociates himself from the still poise of nature and in some deed embodies the sort of desire or willing which we agree to call human, which Pound specifically terms 'ideas in action'. To present these, the mask, to be sure, serves. But there are, it would seem, aspects of the 'idea in action' which the dramatic monologue will not render. To do justice to these aspects Pound has developed a mode which I can only call *declamation*—declamation because in such passages the elements of narrative or drama are always in strict subordination to effects of direct address, of exhortation, effects calculated (it would seem) to sharpen and influence our powers of perception. There is a further difference: the subject-matter of the declaimed sections differs from that of the sheerly imagistic ones not only in being dynamic (an 'idea in action'); no longer does Pound hold up a clear pane of glass. Why indeed should he? The mode of imagism occurs in those sections where statement as statement suffices (physical objects and easily related objects like Ulysses). But sheer statement, when one comes to any action, any section of human, non-'natural' history, does not—*pace* 'scientific history'—suffice. Rather does the poet—whatever his overt desire to continue the mode of disavowal—hold before the declaimed objects a square of glass which (one cannot easily miss this) is coloured: at times the calm blue of peace, at other times the red of anger. Oratory, declamation—these seek to colour whatever they present. It does not suffice (as it does for a natural object) to *report* the activities of a Malatesta (Cantos VIII, IX, and X), of a Frederick II of Hapsburg-Lorraine who reformed the credit-laws of eighteenth-century Florence (Canto XLIV); one does not refer without emotional overtones to the founding of a rational credit-system in seventeenth century Siena (Canto XLII). In short, one does not touch this sort of material without the colouring of approval, without (very often) implications that suggest it is urgent we see why approval is right. And conversely, one does not—at any rate, Pound does not—report peculations in the munitions trade (Cantos XXXVIII and XL) or the throttle-hold of Prussianism on German culture (Cantos XIX and XXXV) without direct, unconcealed accents of disgust and hatred. But—here the line must be drawn firmly—the passages of declamation do not shade into (as they might have in older poetry untouched by Pound's deathly fear of abstractions) passages of explicit statement. The perceived deed, like the perceived image, is not capped by any general, inclusive statement. The urgency of the tone—which does call for public approval, public scorn—our sense of having (in these sections of declamatory presentation) our attention intensely fixed on a fragment of historical narrative or compressed economic explanation, carries forward the process so dear to Pound's heart: the coerced creation, in our minds, of an arch of comment on the poem, an arch of comment more encompassing than the arch the tiny Chinese poem is supposed to coerce—more encompassing but analogous to it.

If a particular reader does not make this response to the device I have called declamation—if, instead, he persists in feeling that he wanders among fragments, then that reader does not profit from the signal which (I argue) Pound gives whenever he takes up the mode declamatory: a signal that says that here is something fairly plain— something to admire, something to detest. (Further, the reader in question has probably set at naught Pound's general method which, recall, he entitles the method of the ideogram: a method that is not an exact imitation of the Chinese method—as are many of Pound's earlier treatments of Chinese originals—but is rather that method altered to operate on the large stage of *The Cantos*, still Chinese in spirit since readers are expected to be moved by exposure not to abstractions but to concrete experiences rendered in words, rendered by the variety of devices we now study.)

Perhaps, it is well to halt at this point in our analysis of specific devices to be reminded of the purpose that they are intended to serve. For from Pound's critical prose, from the poem, one should gather that *The Cantos* cannot be regarded—shall we say?—as a succession of self-divertissements in the modes imagistic, declamatory, or other modes still to be made clear. Rather, we need to remind ourselves, is the poem for Pound a way—*the* way, since ordinary channels of communications are hopelessly polluted—of awakening human beings to the need for 'making things new': making them new, if one is reading *The Cantos*, by braying the confused, miscellaneous stuff of the past in the mortar of the poem. Braying is not a gentle, orderly action; the methods perceptible in *The Cantos* are not gentle and orderly. Thus, those who admire the grace of the sections I call imagistic are doubtless unhappy over the sections here called declamatory. In them, elegance of diction evaporates; language is colloquial, telegraphic, and even (some would say) inept; the movement of the verse is broken up. In fact, the tone is that of prose—prose that exclaims, badgers, often breaks down.

Further, if we concede that Pound's clue was found in Chinese poetry, he follows it far beyond the rendering of specific objects or isolated emotions—follows it to catch, in words, his chosen reality: the sections of cultural history that the reader should be exposed to. When the reader, aware of this, is still distracted by what seem to him extraneous intrusions, he ought to practice a 'suspension of impatience'; if he does so, he will be rewarded (on a second or third reading) by feeling at home, by not being 'put off', whatever device (image or declamation or mask) is suddenly thrust at him. For one may say that each device, each fragment where that device is worked out, exists not for itself but for its possible donation to the over-arching meaning in the mind which the poem is calculated to coerce from the reader. An adequate analogy for all of this is the method of mosaic. If, at Ravenna, one stands too near a wall, one sees the special squares of colour, unblended, individual, unrelatable to the rest of the composition. If, however, one moves away, there emerges— by the fact of visual combination—the distinguished, hieratic excellence of the temple adornments. Let us not insist that the comparison between the labours of the artist in mosaic and those of Pound in words is close. It is not. It would be closer if one were to imagine what would survive the partial bombing of San Vitale. Pound's material— the stuff of human experience—*has* been bombed (he would say) for several centuries by the working of usury, more specifically of capitalistic democracy. From these ruins—the breaking-up of significant, rich human experience—only the dishonest patch together a picture or a poem that is easy to grasp.

Next in our chosen order of explanation—which does not correspond to the order of the poem, though an order, I believe, exists there—come the masks, the personae; but the masks, as I have said, differently employed— employed not as units (they are so employed in Pound's early work) but used always as part of a unity: *The Cantos*. The masks, if we bother to draw up a list, are used (we will find) for a direct—as opposed to the declamatory—presentation of sensibilities and cultures that Pound finds admirable or detestable.

How then do these differ from the earlier personae? How, that is, is one to perceive in them the glints of malice through the eye-slits rather than the mood of disavowal that pervades the earlier personae? The answer, I believe, runs thus and justifies my earlier invocation of both Browning and Landor. Each mask in *The Cantos*, *taken alone* (just as with each imagistic section taken alone), does not seem a wide gulf away from earlier practice. But this, of course, is not the way to deal with *any* element in the poem (as I have shown, for example, in treating the continuation of imagism). Thus, the masks of the admirable persons from the past, when considered collectively, come to exhibit the apertures through which Pound's hatred for the present flashes; and here the malice is not, of course, for the offered masks but for that which has elsewhere received declamatory treatment in what I have called the mood of red, the mood of anger. The masks of the admirable represent various sorts of persons, a helter-skelter crew that has in common one thing only (all are on the angelic side of Pound's guiding usurious, non-usurious dichotomy); this should not surprise, for one must get over depending on more traditional divisions between the saved and the lost. However oddly, the saved and the saving in *The Cantos* range widely, from (for example) the ruthless condottieri Sigismondo to the eminently respectable and controlled John Adams. All we need to recognize is that both men—and the many others instanced —lived apart from usury or protested against it. That Adams was an eighteenth century rationalist and a good family man and that Malatesta was a tyrant and (according to his enemies) an odd sort of husband and father does not in Pound's eyes separate them seriously. Each man realized certain notable human potentialities that cannot be realized under the evil star of usury. The mask of either man, then, held up in relation to or against usury, will (without ceasing to be Malatesta or Adams) allow the contempt, the distaste of the poet, as full expression as is possible on the terms that govern the shaping of the poem.

That Pound uses few masks for the presentation of material from the realm of evil—that he uses for evil, rather, the direct presentation of the declamatory method— may seem to some readers a chance missed. But it was a chance the luxury of which Pound (with his sensibility) could not allow himself. His approach to nearly all his chosen masks is the approach of 'translation' (that is, of complete rendering)—in short, a technique, at the outset, of disavowal. But, as we have seen, Pound could 'disavow' only what in a deeper sense he could avow, only those things and persons that are to him a refuge from the banality and worse of his own age. Usually, in *The Cantos*, when he turns to his own age, he does not 'translate' it into dramatic monologues. He must exhibit it; but he cannot become it as he becomes persons who participated in a happier culture. For his own age—and following Flaubert—he can compose a declamatory *sottisier* from the triviality and perversions it offers (as did Mr. Mencken in the *Americana* section of the old *American Mercury*). But he cannot take these counters of our culture as anything but symbols of degradation and villainy, of conscious or unwitting enmity to the multifarious reality composed by admirable 'ideas in action'—composed by what Mr. Pound would consent to call human. Naturally, similar counters or significant attitudes from relatively blessed ages do not go into a declamatory *sottisier*; rather, they are the very stuff from which the masks are manufactured. Does this bivalent treatment of similar material seem odd? Not if one has perceived that the apparent detachment of *The Cantos* is misleading—that the poem is, at all points, written from love and hate and their interplay. Flaubert might have found it in his heart to exhibit the crudities of a distant culture, and perhaps he did in *Salammbô*; only comprehension was at stake for him. But more than comprehension is at stake in *The Cantos*. The masks, for example, are not held up to move us to comprehension, but to move us to action—to a stirring of the will to imitate what we admire in John Adams, to an attack on the temple of Usuria itself.

One should note, in concluding a discussion of the

masks, that Pound's style in these sections varies widely
but (I think) not erratically. Occasionally there are the
accents of dispassionate nobility that continue the mood
of the Ulysses section. But as a rule, the utterance is
broken and compressed. The diction is often lifted or pretends to be lifted from documentary sources (old letters,
legal depositions, fiscal decrees) and exhibits the sorts of
formality or casualness, the dryness, and the downright
obscurity that one would find in these various sources.
Those who, at this point, pine for the elegance of diction
in the early *Personae* will likely proceed to condemn their
continuation in *The Cantos*, the mask sections, out of
context. *In* context—and that is how one must at least
begin in forming an answer to a question as to the effectiveness of a certain device—one can discount the unpoetic
immediate effect (the tedium inhering in much of the John
Adams mask, the legal gobblydegook which is the verbal
integument of Malatesta) and instead concede that the
presentation is aligned with Pound's expressed purpose of
exhibiting 'ideas in action'. Not, note, 'ideas in action' as
they *ought* to be after being worked over by the idealizing
romantic poet (one thinks of Schiller's marmoreal Joan
of Arc) but as they were in 'reality' or, at least, in the
poet's contrived equivalent of the rough, unlicked moment
or person from the past: moments and persons that, to a
careless view, lacked significance or direction. Thus each
mask—by its irregularity of rhythm, by its diction frequently vapid or limping—indicates that *this* is the form
even the greatest 'ideas in action' had. Even so, mixtures
of tedium with direction and vigour only intermittent,
these rendered 'ideas in action' are the best that mortal
man may hope for, within the limits that Pound lays out
(myth, religions, the oversoul—these words refer to matters,

ranges of experience, that are for Pound out of bounds).

Thus, it is seen that the form and diction one finds in the mask sections record a deviation from the mood that governed the creation of the early *Personae*. There, thanks to narrow limits, thanks to Pound's utter preoccupation with 'translation' *per se*, the poet could concentrate on a sort of excellence that he willingly sabotages in the mask sections in *The Cantos*. Why this sabotage? Because, as I have said, in *The Cantos* the masks have a function in relation to the rest of the poem. Indeed, if they had more point, more finish in themselves (that is, polish, unity, and obvious direction), they would have less point for the rest of the poem. So polished, so unified, they would then operate for the rest of the poem as Platonic abstractions, emanations or idealizations of human activity that float ineffective, if beautiful, above the muddied stream of life: life, that shapeless congeries of 'ideas in action'. But as they are, the mask sections remain in life: unlovely, 'unpoetical', instinct (perhaps) with the human—with, that is, the groping as well as the inspired. They are 'emblems' to remind us of what man is—or, at least, in less perverted ages, has been. But they must never become elements in a composite picture of ideal man; did they ever have this hateful effect, that would be to betray men: men, whose existence across the centuries is one of the few demonstrable facts—men, whom Pound would betray if he allowed his poem the transformation scene from fairyland that takes place when we stop talking about specific men stumbling through specific existences and commence speaking fatuously of man who, doubtless, moves effortlessly from one level of being to another.

The next device which the conscientious reader of *The Cantos* has to estimate and be ready to respond to properly

is Pound's use of pronouns: far from the trivial matter
that mere mention here suggests. Throughout the poem
there is a curious use of pronouns that has nothing to do
with the use of the first person dramatic, where the relation
of the first person to the other persons is no source of
dubiety. The use—or uses—I now have in mind occurs in
the sections I have called declamatory: sections, that is,
that are non-dramatic, that are either narrative or exposition,
compressed, jagged, hortatory. This use one may first
judge simply accidental and irritating; one comes, later,
to see it as one of the most curious 'machines' in the poem
—indeed, the most 'original' one in that its very existence
is not—like the mode imagistic and the use of the mask—
a continuation and modification of methods not invented
for *The Cantos*. Even more than the mode declamatory to
which it is attached is this use of pronouns a product of
what Pound conceives to be the all-over procedure of the
poem: the method of the ideogram, a method which
amounts to a rough, continuous juxtaposition of unarti-
culated elements, a method which is expected to produce
in the reader an emergent judgment that the poet, leery of
facile abstraction, refuses to provide. The use of the
pronouns intensifies at many points the sense of
urgent pressure which the practice of juxtaposition has
set up.

Yet here again the person who has come to know *The
Cantos* by stages (a kind of acquaintance that the process
of the publication of the poem has encouraged) may glide
past this problem without recognizing it as one that is
susceptible to isolation and discussion. True, he cannot
avoid observing the existence of unimplemented pronouns;
but he is likely to write them off as one more inscrutable
cause of confusion. They may cause confusion (it is not

the purpose of this essay to presume to explain away the confusion of the poem, but simply to reduce that confusion to its proper proportion); but they are not, these unimplemented pronouns, inscrutable. Given proper scrutiny, they make a hard, definite contribution to one's reading of the poem; like the other devices considered, they in their turn thrust the mind toward what is, for Pound, the wished-for conclusion.

One may say, then, that Pound aims, in the declamatory sections, at establishing not *one* relation with our consciousness but several; further, each of these relations is a different *sort* of assault on our attention, a demand that it be exercised in a way unlike that in which it has been stirred by some other declamatory section. The more numerous the sorts of attention, the more complicated will be their interplay. The more complicated their interplay, the closer will be our approach to portions of the 'reality' Pound exhibits in his poem. (The approach here created would be unsuitable, if not impossible, in the imagistic and mask sections. The device of the mask limits strictly the use of pronouns; and the persistence of the mode of disavowal in the imagistic sections would not be enriched by the juggling with pronouns now in question, for—in *The Cantos* at least—what is disavowed is admired actually. There is a great simplicity to Pound's admirations; effects of suspension, ambiguity, and ironical weighing (the effects of the unimplemented pronouns) are not called for when nature and man are being simply venerated—far too simply, I shall suggest in my last essay. Pound's hatreds may be simple also. But they are also vehement and so seek as many lines of attack as possible, lateral and rear as well as frontal.)

The pronouns, as I analyze their use, are used in four or

five different ways (my identifying terms are barbarous, but they will be seen to be quite precise).

1. The *un*modern pronoun.
2. The modern pronoun.
3. The modernizing pronoun.
4. The unlocalized pronoun.
5. The pronoun of specific address.

I begin with the unmodern pronoun since it is nearest to what does not mystify at all: the use of pronouns in the sections of dramatic monologue. There, all pronouns derive their triangulation simply and naturally from the identity of the recognized speaker and those he is supposed to address. Indeed, the difficulty of this first unimplemented pronoun (as, in differing ways, of the others) consists of this necessity: the reader must search for the points of triangulation. Thanks to the *I, we, you,* and *they* in dramatic monologue, we easily share the experience which an historical figure is familiar with. But there are many sections that are not monologue—that are, instead, monologue (the actual historical 'idea in action') in the process of becoming declamation (the poet's own recital of what the 'idea in action' was). To be precise, the pronouns *we* and *they* appear; but they do not stand for a group of persons that we can actually name, as we can Malatesta or his foes. These pronouns stand instead for the collective consciousness of persons who lived at a certain time.

Thus, when Pound has cause to approach the benign regime of Leopold of Hapsburg-Lorraine in eighteenth-century Tuscany, there occurs this passage in which the pronoun *our* is used to tie down, to moor this section of non-dramatic exposition.

    Leopold cut down the debt interest
and put the Jesuits out
                and put end to the Inquisition
1782
    and they brought in Mr. Locke's
essay on interest
          but Genoa took our trade and Livorno
kept treaty with England to the loss of Livorno
that is to say Livorno trade took a loss . . .
                  (Canto L.)

The effect of *our* (and of the invidious reference to the opposed *they*) is that we are put into a direct, naive relationship with the material. We put aside our own *arrière-pensées* which are the gifts, good and bad, of our own time. We not only take up our places in the collective, ordinary, and utterly undistinguished life of another time; we achieve the overtones of response proper to that distant time, and we lose touch with the overtones proper to our own time. In a word, we become unmodern; we divest ourselves of our awareness of living in the twentieth century. We undergo an alteration of consciousness that Pound distinctly does not wish us to undergo at many other places in the poem, since in those places the pathos or irony is contingent on our preserving (in the oddest of contexts) the *arrière-pensées* proper to our section of history. But such a cherishing (if one may cherish what is contemptible) must be avoided in the sections where the unmodern pronoun appears—as, at first reading, they (the overtones of the present) must also be put aside in the dramatic monologues. What Pound calls 'translation' (effective mastery of the texts or even the culture of another age) must be complete if the block of verse which constitutes the ideograms now in question is to be vigorous in impact. We must, that is, read without irony. Or if that is impossible,

74

we must delay as long as possible the dawn of a sense of irony—a sense which arises, as is habitual in *The Cantos*, from the relating of an historical figure or (with the unmodern pronoun sections) an historical collectivity to our leaders or to ourselves. If the irony is to be finally intense, we must begin by forgetting that we are twentieth-century men. We must have, if the verse avail, direct experience of living uncritically and receptively in some other period.

The second sort of unimplemented pronoun is what I call the modern pronoun. Its effect is the opposite of the one just discussed in that it causes us to share in some phase of the operation of the modern collective consciousness. But its effect is immediately and obviously that of irony: irony that springs from an inclusive loathing. Pound can approach the historically distant collective consciousness with beautiful dispassion (have we not suggested that, in *The Cantos*, continuation of the 'mode of disavowal' signifies the strongest kind of avowal?). He cannot approach the modern collective consciousness without the strongest stirrings of repudiating hatred; what other emotion is possible whenever we walk in the realms of usury? Hatred may be muted in the passage which I turn to; but one feels its maleficent vibrato.

The passage concerns a visit made to a decayed mansion: a mansion built in the nineteenth century when the merchant princes—slaves to ostentation though they were—tried to scant paying the full price true magnificence exacts, and settled for the gaudy, the deceptive, and the second-rate. In the course of Pound's report, these lines occur:

> We also made ghostly visits, and the stair
> That knew us, found us again on the turn of it,
> Knocking at empty rooms, seeking for buried beauty;

And the sun-tanned, gracious and well-formed fingers
Lift no latch of bent bronze, no Empire handle
Twists for the knocker's fall; no voice to answer.
                                        (Canto VII.)

We and *us* indicate that we are to think of ourselves as
present—physically, morally present—in the old house
just as (thanks to the pronouns in the Leopold passage)
we are rendered physically and morally present in the
benign Florence that was shattered by Napoleon and
Metternich. The modern pronouns, to repeat, demand our
participation in some modern event, and we participate as
component elements of a typical, unindividuated group;
only as members of that group do we function—we may
not detach ourselves as we go through a section of banality
that is not new. But the poet's diction and accent give the
show away at once; as part of the collective *we*, we are
plainly frustrate, incomplete. Plainly, life comes to very
little indeed as we move within the construct which exists
in the usurious present as a shabby substitute for earlier
sorts of collective life that were—imperfectly but definitely
—human. All the collective *we* is allowed is a mimicking of
the motions of being human, of responding to delight and
pain. In lines like the following, we have but the partial
existence, the stunted responses of sleep-walkers:

So we sat there, with the old kindly professor,
And the stubby little man was up-stairs.
And there was the slick guy in the other
corner reading *The Tatler* . . . (Canto XIX.)

The next pronoun, what I call the modernizing pronoun,
is not to be equivalated, in its effects, with the modern
pronoun just discussed. Sections in which the modernizing
pronoun appears always associate a pronoun of unindicated

antecedent with a past age. But (the context assures) this pronoun cannot refer to the collective consciousness of another age (that is what the unmodern pronoun does). It stands, instead, for the consciousness of present man— present man detached from the collective, sullied consciousness to which the modern pronoun refers; present man, cultivated and aware of all that has happened to him; present man turning to another age and, as he turns, carrying with him all his burden of *arrière-pensées* that experience and taste and study have piled up. It is this kind of consciousness—a consciousness suffering from the tyranny of a usurious culture but not subscribing to it— that is called upon in many declamatory passages that have to do with past ages or (as here) a tessellation of past ages. Thus, in Canto IV, the modernizing pronoun occurs after certain wide-ranging references. There is a reference to 'old Ecbatan' where 'lay the god's bride, lay ever, waiting for the rain . . .'; and this figure merges with other figures also hierarchical in effect: a religious procession, the stamping of a Centaur's hoof—'ideas in action' either in full correspondence with nature or connected with actions fully human and not inhibited. In this context appears the brief phrase, a phrase that closes the Canto:

> And we sit here . . .
>   there in the arena . . .

In this and similar passages, the unimplemented pronoun is introduced to coerce effects irony or pathos. 'There in the arena' are non-usurious aspects of life, historically distant from us but (we as instructed intelligences cannot fail to sense) instinct with the sort of life, the sort of experience, that is well-nigh impossible for us. 'And we sit here'— sit bound by the bondage peculiar to our age. Here, *we* does not—as does an unmodern pronoun—exist to plunge us more deeply, more richly, into an age non-usurious. It exists to draw us up sharply from the contemplation of what charms and enriches. It lifts us into our own age; it 'modernizes' us unceremoniously and quite brutally. It makes us aware of the juicelessness of our own age; it demands—by the sign-manual of the pronoun itself—that certain contexts be so read, so interpreted. This reading, as we continue or repeat the contact with admirable ages created by certain sections of declamation, will 'spoil' (by coerced over-tones of irony and regret) what ought otherwise to delight us. (A similar example appears at the end of Canto L, where the phrase, 'only we two have moved', invokes the instructed modern consciousness to operate retroactively on what the Canto has presented.)

It should now appear why so extended a discussion of the manipulation of unimplemented pronouns is necessary, why one reads *The Cantos* badly if he carelessly ignores the pronoun signals ... if, for example, he gives irony its play when it is supposed to be suppressed; if (as just now) he does not ask why the relation of *we*, standing for sensitive modern consciousness, to distant periods provides ironic instruction.

Two further uses of pronouns remain; they differ from the three just identified by being but weakly localized in time or place. The modern and unmodern pronouns assign one to a time-level; the modernizing pronoun operates in terms of time-levels. Careless reading will confuse this last use with the one now to be taken up, what I term the unlocalized pronoun. The modernizing pronoun is not really without locus; rather, its entire effect depends upon forcing us to exist in two periods (and sometimes more than two). The unlocalized pronoun exists to evoke an awareness that is detached from all time-sequences. I suppose, as a matter of fact, that it is localized to this extent: it does appeal to one sort of modern consciousness. But it does not concern the modern consciousness collectively expressed (and therefore mediocre and uncritical); nor does it try for the effects of juxtaposition that the modernizing pronoun creates. In short, it concerns the consciousness either of the 'good' reader or of Pound himself. We can say justly that it is unlocalized in that it has already seen the pitch which Usura daubs on our century and has taken steps to divest itself of the stains; it is, in a word, well on the way to the process to which Pound applies the Chinese ideogram that means: 'Making things new.' This consciousness—and the pronouns that call it forth—exists, true, in the twentieth century; but it has ceased to be thoughtlessly enslaved by thus existing. It does not have to be jarred loose from the channels of thought acceptable to capitalist-democracy; it has already left them and is seeking—and perhaps has found—proper channels: proper in that, relative at least to those of capitalist-democracy, they are human.

Therefore, in sections that contain the unlocalized pronoun, the appeal is to the fully cognizant: persons who are aware of the 'drift' of *The Cantos*, who have taken up the proper attitude of repudiation, who know that modern society must be torn down and then built anew: built anew with proper deference to what human-ness is, what ranges of expression must be provided for it. The unlocalized pronouns do not generate antique consciousness or mediocre modern consciousness. The alertness they demand is the completest possible alertness to what is in progress. Those who occupy the steps of Diocletian's palace misunderstand nothing that the poet declaims.

    And we sit here
                under the wall,
    Arena romana, Diocletian's, les gradins
        quarante-troi rangées en calcaire. (Canto XII.)

Thus begins a canto which presents a good many of the
deformations of human instinct under usury. The pronoun
is, as usual, a signal: a signal to which we must respond
properly. And here, the pronoun is of the unlocalized sort.
Our sitting on the steps of Diocletian's palace is not localiz-
ing at all. The supposed situation of *we* is really a counter
that announces that, on what follows, the consciousness
that must operate is that which has been formed and refined
by wide acquaintance with culture past and present. It is,
as I have said, wider and more refined than that appealed to
by the first three pronouns. The consciousness stirred by
the unmodern pronoun is happily immersed in a relatively
good culture; the consciousness stirred by the modern
pronoun is immersed in an evil culture but is too dull to
note anything beyond a vague discomfort; and the consciousness set in motion by the modernizing pronoun—
moving uneasily from age to age—is not awakened or
enlightened (rather, it is in process of moving toward the
enlightenment that *we*, lounging in the palace ruins, firmly
possess). *We* have made all our juxtapositions, our investigations and experiments; these have produced, in Pound,
in us, the unlocalized consciousness that is (one may say)
the court of final appeal in this poem.

    In passages of this nature, the division to be drawn
between *we* (the fully conscious readers) and *I* (supposedly
Pound) is not so sharp as one might (reading so imperious
a poet) expect. Elsewhere, it is true, we must be content
to be Pound's pupils; but here we, the 'good' readers, are
conceived of as the poet's equals. And since we are his

equals in *this* context, Pound does not draw a line between his consciousness and ours; *I* and *we* serve the same purpose, that of appealing to the highest court, the enlightened consciousness possessed by us and Pound. Very seldom does Pound employ *I* in a sense personal rather than, in my terminology, unlocalized. (Canto XX, p. 89, contains an example of a sheerly personal use of *I*; Pound is speaking of a visit he made to a savant in search of learning. But even this passage has implications that are wider than the biographical.) But usually *I*, like *we*, is an alerting of the full, disenchanted, dissociated consciousness. Thus emancipated, unlocalized, the judging, sorting mind profits from the vantage-point it has taken up; it wears garments as clean of Usury's pitch as may be, and it sees as far as human eye may see. (The 'good' reader and Pound are not fools enough to try to see farther.)[1]

This explicit consideration given to the protean behaviour of pronouns should warn a reader not to look for (if, at this point, he is still looking) any unity of tone or delivery in the poem. Thus, each section of declamation—like the sections considered earlier, those of monologue or those that continue the imagistic mode, has a tone proper to its use of pronoun. In fact, it butters Pound's bread to have the tones so unlike that we will not have cause to confuse one sort of counter or ideogram (in Pound's developed sense) with another.

Pound, in his criticism, often speaks of the three-fold source of strength in poetry: melopoeia, phanopoeia, and logopoeia. He defines these as the related arts of using

[1] I do not think it worth while to go beyond identifying the pronoun of direct address, used by Pound to invoke the attention not of some portion of the reader's consciousness but of some economist or critic. Here one finds a continuation of the harangues that are a feature of Pound's prose; there is nothing obscure in their intention or import.

sound, of projecting images, and (the special skill adhering to the art that employs words) of exploiting the complexity of language itself. Melopoeia we have touched in passing, and the projecting of the image concerns, I should imagine, the rendering of specific natural objects and 'ideas in action'. If I am right, of this second sort of 'device' we have spoken sufficiently. And what is logopoeia but the succession of 'devices', their often puzzling alternation, that we have observed carefully in speaking of the 'masks' and the unimplemented pronouns? Yet four aspects of what Pound calls logopoeia remain; and they are, for full understanding of *The Cantos*, crucial ones. For they abet the 'masks' and the shifts in the declamatory sections indicated by the pronouns in coercing from the consciousness of the reader the proper over-arching of meaning. The four remaining aspects of logopoeia, then, are these: diction, repetition, juxtaposition of elements, and the general plan.

Thus far, in making certain things as plain as may be, I have suggested sharp divisions between unlike elements. These divisions exist, but there is in the poem an effect of blending, of insistence on inter-relationships—an effect established by Pound's use of language. I have already spoken of the somewhat haranguing tone of the declaimed sections and the 'elevated' tone of the sheer imagist section that celebrate nature *as* nature; nor do I need to identify the mood of elegy in the lament for the victims of usury or the unrestrained vituperation for the usurers in hell. These varieties of diction belong to isolatable sections; they demand no special preparation on the part of the reader, nor do the dramatic monologues, once the basic convention is perceived (that is, the use of the banal diction of chance talk, the reproduction of the dry dust of legal documents and state papers—both exist to put the 'idea in action'

THE DEVICES OF POUND'S *CANTOS*

into real, valid movement). What the reader does need to note are certain (at first glance) erratic deviations from the established, comprehensible tones or textures just listed.

These are the deviations that (for some readers) shatter the pleasure of what would conventionally be called 'good passages'. It is quite easy to say *what* is done, what (in way of diction) goes against a locally established grain of language. There are parodies of foreign use of English, sudden appearances of English and American dialects, the intrusion of slang and neologisms into historical monologues and declamatory passages on historical themes, sudden deviations into Greek or Latin or Provencal, burlesques of recognized and ridiculous styles of expression. It is, I say, quite easy to say *what* is done. And one can hope to suggest *why* these deviations endlessly occur: the deviations which seem to shatter an effect, a mood about to be firmly established.

Is the poem at this point—the manipulation of an immense variety of diction-levels—masterless? Hardly, I think. Rather is all that I have noted a species of logopoeia; it is a play of mind over material which the very nature of language encourages in those who have perceived the fullness and complexity of that nature. Thus, the variety and 'unevenness' constitute an assertion of mastery—an assertion that *The Cantos* is one poem and not a collection of poems scarcely related to each other, one poem that has for its subject the expression (within the limits of the ideogram as defined by Pound) of the most important conflict that study and experience present a modern writer: the usury, non-usury dichotomy. Thus, the frequent banter and slang, the inserted and deflating irreverence for what has been done seriously, compose an ironical appeal to us—the enlightened readers, the readers sometimes specifically appealed to by the unlocalized pronouns, to exercise our full powers. This is not difficult when there is a sustained parody of antique or legal language (as in many a section of dramatic monologue) or when the accent of Webster or of Lord North's servant is burlesqued. What perplexes, what challenges justification or rejection, is the intrusion of these same effects into sections of declamation. What is gained here—in the monologues, for that matter?

This: the effect of complete 'translation'. The passages which suffer, in the geological sense, a 'thrust' from another level of language usage are nearly always those which deal with the past. At least, colloquialisms and slang do not, naturally, disturb the reader when they appear in modern contexts. But whenever these effects startle, one should not rest with finding them wilful. Pound, in speaking of attempts to translate Aeschylus, has brutal contempt for the 'pretty', pseudo-archaic, or periphrastic qualities he finds in the various translations of the Greek dramatist. (Similarly, he dubs the Lang, Leaf, and Myers translation of Homer a Biblical regurgitation.) A translation, however complete, can never be the original (nor can the re-creation of an age be the same as the age when it existed). A translation is much more likely to be nearly complete or satisfactory if the translator does not ignore the limitations of the foreign language and of his own; rather, he should capitalize on the differences, the gaps between the two languages, as well as seek out the similarities. Whenever Pound, in his criticism, praises a translation, he has perceived that the translator worked with differences as well as similarities in mind. A translation cannot aspire to catch the alien excellence of the original; it should—in its free use of colloquialism, slang, and current reference— say: 'Translation made for our present purposes only.' (Hence, Pound's praise for Douglas's Aeneid, Golding's Metamorphoses, and Andreas Divus's Latin version of Homer.) 'Our present purposes' when we read the historical sections of *The Cantos* are not greatly unlike our purposes when we seek out a modern translation of a classic work: in either instance, we hope to establish and maintain a fruitful relationship between ourselves and that which is distant. Thus, diction in Pound's poem which startles us by its apparent irrelevance is there to make certain that our stance vis-à-vis Malatesta or John Adams and their eras will yield us something more galvanic than the archaically pretty. What is called 'historical fiction' seldom comes to more than the charmingly distracting; whatever really startling charge a past age might hold for us is kept from us by the insulating operation of a uniform, removed diction. If the past is to be made really capable of shocking us, of making us see what another age was and what our age distinctly is not, we must use—or as readers, become accustomed to—a diction which revives for us, at our particular point in history, the roughness as well as the glories of a time that has receded in history; we must be reminded, as ever, of the gulf that exists between us and a good many other ages. Thus, when Pound imitates in a Malatesta section a 'dago' pronunciation of English, he does so not at the cost of the Renaissance Italians; we are reminded, midway in the pageant of old magnificence, of our easy condescension for 'dagoes'—men who are the distant products, whose 'foreignness' testifies to the workings, of a culture we do not equal.

The completest 'translation' is, in *The Cantos*, dependent on the creation and maintenance of the completest cross reference possible. There must be a sense (whatever the particular topic at hand) of reference made to the sum-total of experience (of taste and study) shared by the poet and his 'good' readers. In Pound's poem, visits to this and that past are not antiquarian. We follow the whole course of Chinese history because we and Pound are passionately interested in modern history, our history. We make the acquaintance of John Adams because he is a man whose experience instructs. With these and a host of similar observations in mind, we may say that, though *The Cantos* may well get out of hand for some readers, they do not get out of hand for Mr. Pound. Faith that this is so is, I think, generated by prolonged acquaintance with the poem, even if we do not possess absolute certainty as to the precise reason for every irrelevance or every lapse from a given level of diction. Indeed, further study often does permit one to see what a previous lapse announced, how it works (if obscurely) to remind one of the dichotomy and draws the loose web of the poem a little tighter.[1]

This function of diction leads one easily to repetition, the establishment of cross-reference not by tone of intruded diction but by the brute fact of intruded subject-matter. The first is an implied reference to sorts of consciousness worked out fully in other ideogram blocks; the second is a stated reference. Two references to the fashion of eating with gold forks (in Venice of the Doges, in nineteenth-century New York) demand that one compare the two blocks of experience involved, suggest that one ask whether the identical facts (the gold forks) have the same meaning in the two contexts. (They do not; Venetian magnificence was vulgar and perfectly human—New York magnificence was vulgar and bare of human import.) When the

---

[1] The sort of diction I treat here is totally absent from two sorts of sections: one, the fairly frequent and nostalgic reconstructions of the rites and joys: of the ancient world and of nature in the ancient world; two, the often mentioned (and unique) lament for the world despciled by usury. Perhaps with this last, one should associate the hell-section, which has no intrusions either.

Merovingian money-term, the dinar, is used in a Chinese context, one knows that one has moved into an approved section of history; Charlemagne's 'commodity dollar' receives the sanctions of the Chinese conclusions independently arrived at. The relations of contrast or of similarity that I have perceived in the forks and the dinar repetitions are, of course, constructions coerced in the mind of the reader; they are not worked out by Pound. Such workings-out smack of the realm of abstract statement—a realm, recall, that is for Pound the ante-chamber to that occupied by the usuriously damned.

This repetition takes place only at fairly long intervals. Its opposite, juxtaposition (the association from canto to canto or within a single canto of opposed or apparently unrelated elements or blocks of ideograms) is perhaps the fundamental method of procedure in the poem, the ground-bass to which we have thus far been considering the counter-point, the obscurely managed harmonies. It has the effect of first straining to the limit minds made torpid by the facile rhetoric of our culture which demands of writers a parade of ideas that are arranged according to expectation or custom and that troop by so docilely that attention is never arrested. Later, the constant juxtaposition, the shift from one topic to another, may restore the 'tone' of the flaccid minds—may transform bad readers (readers that await predigested ideas) into 'good' readers, readers capable of co-operating with the poet in ways already specified. To such 'good' readers, the juxtapositions are usually understandable, make some point (great or little) about the general dichotomy that is the subject of the poem. Yet certain kinds of juxtaposition take on clarity in light of the division Pound sees between our age and most others. In rereading, one perceives that what seemed at first to be

elements utterly diverse are bound together by one circumstance and one alone: they belong to ages that are
pre-usurious. Or, in other cantos, shards and tatters of
our own culture agglomerate with usury as their focus.
Further, one may say that the mechanism of juxtaposition
operates to create close parallels or flat contrasts; the
juxtapositions of subject-matter never occur to make us
perceive shades of difference or shades of similarity. 'He
who is not with me is against me.' The 'good' reader comes
to see that his palate is expected to do one of two things:
accept joyfully or spew forth.

Finally, from one's all-over reading—a reading backward
and forward, a reading that struggles to keep in touch
with as much of the poem as possible—comes a sense of a
kind of all-over plan. Perhaps I have insisted too flatly
that thus and so are the natures of the earlier items I
group under Pound's heading of logopoeia; if so, let me
concede that not all all-over plans—that is, the perceptions in
separate readers of the 'drift' of the poem from start to
present halt—would be identical. But the separate perceptions would, I think, note some of the elements and the
arrangements that I shall note now. The early cantos make
a statement about the purity of nature and the Greeks, the
comparative purity of the Renaissance. Then come the
hell of modern life and the literal hell of the usurers; and
these two themes with proper illustrations continue for
some space their alternation, with interludes concerned
with non-usurious cultures. What one can note (previous
to the commencement of the Chinese section) is that each
ideogram block is larger and more weighty than similar
blocks earlier in the poem. This looming larger of each
topic touched prepares one for the giving of many cantos
(and not, as at the outset, portions of a canto only) to one

subject: first, a declamatory section that is in effect a history of China; second, monologue-cum-declamation devoted to John Adams. These two groups, if appearing early in the poem, would amount to a reversal of method. Not so in their present position; they culminate. For China affords us the 'demonstration' of a country whose history often responds to something sound (the Ta Hio of Confucius); and the life of John Adams offers us the spectacle of a man who fought to remain sound in a world that responded to what was corrupt: the transformation of real goods into money and credits. The latest—and perhaps concluding—section, *The Pisan Cantos*, composed in a prison camp without access to source materials, has the effect of a coda. There is a return to the compressed juxtaposition of the earlier cantos; and the themes that are by now familiar are closely intertwined with two sorts of biographical material: Pound's recollections of contacts and conflicts that led to clarification of his view of the world and the writing of *The Cantos*, and his notation of the physically present scene (the tent, the improvised table, etc.) that says for him and for his readers: 'The demonstration is complete; the case is closed.'

Perhaps readers who have Pound's familiarity with early music, with its deceptive clarity, with its elegances of suspension and recapitulation, of retardation of theme and flashing short-cut to a goal, will have still more to say of the all-over arrangement of the ideogram blocks. With this suggestion I conclude my analysis of Pound's 'logopoeia' and the other devices which the poet exploits in *The Cantos*. It is a poem that, like Spenser's, exhibits a double order—the sequential order just now touched on, and the more important order: the use of the devices or the rhetorical emblems which give the reader the 'leads' he may properly hope to find. But there is a difference also. In Spenser, one may master the order of events— the equivalent of the sequential order I have just discussed —without bothering with the devices of Spenser's poem, the complex allegory. But in *The Cantos*, a full perception waits upon a mastery of the rhetoric, the devices, of the poem. Perception of these must (as in this essay) come first.

Nor may they be perceived for their own sake. As I have said elsewhere, *The Cantos* is a poem with a purpose. For in several places—Cantos XXX, XXXVI, XLV, LI, LXXIX, LXXXI—Pound drops his masks, abandons his devices, and speaks of his purposes in accents that have no place in any well-arranged ideogram. I quote the conclusion of one of these direct, unveiled laments.

> Usura slayeth the child in the womb
> It stayeth the young man's courting
> It hath brought palsey to bed, lyeth
> between the young bride and her bridegroom
> CONTRA NATURAM
> They have brought whores for Eleusis
> Corpses are set to banquet
> at behest of usura. (Canto XLV.)

And one of the last cantos ends with a comment on the poem—and perhaps on Pound's career outside the poem —that could not be more explicit.

> To have gathered from the air a live tradition
> or from a fine eye the unconquered flame
> This is not vanity.
> Here error is all in the not done,
> all in the diffidence that faltered. (Canto LXXXI.)

But the canto that follows such a flat asseveration is likely to begin with a denial that reveals Pound's uneasiness at having been moved to direct expression, to the sort of general statement whose simulacra are propped up in the temples of Usura. The outbreak of Canto XLV is followed by this warning to those who are hasty in deciding what *The Cantos* 'means'.

> And if you will say that this tale teaches . . .
> a lesson, or that the Reverend Eliot
> has found a more natural language . . . you who think
>   you will
> get through hell in a hurry . . . (Canto XLVI.)

In Pound's view, those who think they will get through hell in a hurry will not get through hell at all; they will merely —along with their preceptors—deceive themselves.

Perhaps we have a measure of the real heat of Pound's conviction in that he puts aside, not once but several times in his poem, his chosen and (he believes) necessary method. It is as though his hatred of capitalist-democracy makes him forget his fear of any or all sorts of general statement. So moved, he permits himself, if briefly, the privilege that his rhetorical theory and practice extend not to the poet but to the reader: the privilege of perceiving and *uttering* the over-arching meaning that is supposed to be the creation of the reader, not of the poet. These breakings-forth suggest that *The Cantos* is more than an annunciation to be accepted in silence and pondered in the heart. They suggest, rather, that the poem and its total import, though hedged about like a sacred grove with prohibitions, exist to be profanced. The poem and its import exist to be weighed and measured not only as poetry but as the particular urgencies felt by a particular man of this century.

RECKONING

T HE *CANTOS*, we have suggested, is a poem that interests in many connections. It is the capital piece of 'evidence' in any dispute between Ezra Pound and the United States government. Literarily, it cannot be regarded as a 'sport', a wilful driving of the language in the direction of obscurity and inconsecutiveness. It is rather—in respect to technique—the investigation of the resources of our language when manipulated in an unusual way: a way that Pound was driven to discover as an alternative to communication that is orderly, logical, and (in Pound's opinion) bootless.

If we have been successful in doing this much, in establishing these points, we have done a good deal for that complex of facts—Ezra Pound and *The Cantos*—that has puzzled many earnest people. However, the previous essays are but preparatory to a precise consideration of the 'complex' itself. At this point, certain things should be clear. We know what the poem attempts and what it does not attempt. We see that there are *different* techniques of confusion in our culture, techniques that the facile reader lumps together. We see that it is uncritical to identify a technique that is invented and perfected in the interest of renewing our language and culture (Pound's technique in *The Cantos*) with techniques which, at points, it may resemble. These other techniques may prove, on inspection, to be no more than verbal gestures that express despair or cynicism in the face of our cultural crisis. They may record—as readers of much recent poetry know—the poet's sense that he is utterly apart—in himself and in his peculiar and injured sensitivity—from the great panorama of destruction that is our time. At any rate, his poem will be a record—more or less confusing in technique—of what it is for one person to live through a troubled age; his poem may even be a gesture of resignation in the face of what is too great for him to think of mastering. Study of such work would doubtless be complete at the point which we have now reached in our study of Pound; for if no more than personal revelation is supposed or guessed to inhere in a poem, 'justice' is done it when one has pointed out the probable sources of the malaise and the peculiar use of language which is useful to the poet in registering or alleviating this malaise. One may say that, for such a poet, the writing of a poem is fundamentally expression and only incidentally communication.

It is not so with Pound. The writing of *The Cantos* is at least as much communication as expression. True, it would not have been written save for the deep discomforts, the intense impatiences, that we have already identified as the fruit of Pound's immediate and personal contact with capitalist-democracy. He never lets us forget that the times are out of joint. Nor does he let us forget what is more important: that if the times are to be set to rights, it is he and his poem that very likely will do it.

It is because of this optimism—an optimism marked by old wounds but doggedly pursuing success within very constricted limits—that analysis may not stop at this point. (It is a point at which the general outlines of a correct apprehension of what the problems are have been drawn in—a point which makes more certain the ultimate profit of investigations of Pound's manipulation of his sources and his modifications of the poetic rhetoric that existed when he began to write.) Optimistic after its fashion, Pound's poem aims at communication; the effect expected of it is that, by the act of communication, it will modify the 'paideuma', the cluster of custom and idea to which we attach ourselves uncritically. Our reckoning of *The Cantos* involves us not only in treatment of the poem itself but also in estimates of its value as an attack on the crucial ailment of our time. The ailment, recall, may be phrased thus, in language that is in line with Pound's own angle of approach: there is a great defect in the inner 'go' of our culture; and it is a defect that will not be offset by conferences, treaties, and pacts—nor yet by the pulpit exhortations of the frocked and of the non-frocked in 'learneries'. That Pound has addressed himself to this huge task leads us to execute a further act of judgment that would not be at all necessary were *The Cantos* chiefly a self-gratifying act of skill. This act of judgment involves answering the following questions. Does the method of the ideogram— the striving to put to work in English (and at an exceedingly complex task) a mode of communication that Pound first perceived in Chinese poetry—actually produce the communication that Pound desiderates? Effective or not, to what general tendency in modern culture may Pound's chosen mode of communication be linked? (To be sure, Pound's tone suggests that his chosen mode is unique, a new departure in our culture. Of this claim in particular we need to be sceptical.) Finally, is what Pound does communicate as full of meat as he thinks it is? Does it—this proffered aggregate of insights—actually constitute a really impressive prologomena to the labours of renewing our culture?

Does it, by the light it casts on dark reaches of our experience, teach us to walk better than we walk at present?

Doubtless when one falls (as here) to speaking of what a poem communicates and of how it acts (or fails to act) as a fulcrum, one falls into what two American critics (W. K. Wimsatt and M. C. Beardsley) have called 'the intentional fallacy'. It is indeed wise to be on one's guard at two related points: reckless and subjective speculation about what a poet's intention might have been, and the uncritical acceptance of the poet's own account of the intention that lay behind the writing of a certain poem. Neither clue should be regarded as the final measure of the worth and the effect of a finished poem. Yet it is also true that the *effect* of a finished poem is no more than a product of the subjective response of a reader and that the first framing of a poem was indeed done in terms of some sort of intent. Any judgment of a poem like *The Cantos* must be very incomplete indeed if it does not run the risk of 'the intentional fallacy'. So if I err in what follows, I err wittingly. It is apparent that the subject of this essay is not *The Cantos*, the poem for its own sake, cut free of the ties that link it to the poet and the age in which both we and the poet live. This study, it is plain, is concerned throughout with *The Cantos* as an important part of a phenomenon that is both complex and instructive: a 'composed' triad made up of three terms—Pound, his poem, and us as elements in an age. The meaning of any one of these items is impoverished when it is detached from the other two. I do not deny that in the sections of this essay devoted to comprehension—and not to judgment, as is this essay—I have tried to isolate both Pound and his poem for special consideration. Further, I have related the poem to Pound's hopes for its ultimate success and to

Pound's own statements about the methods he employs. If these are faults, let this section redress the wrong. Let it insist that Pound's account of what his poem is supposed to be and how it ought to operate do not constitute a complete statement of what the poem actually is. In fact, Pound's account must be 'corrected' by answers to the following questions. Is the ideogram-method actually effective in English? What place does Pound occupy in the traditional picture of Western thought? What is the actual moral and political illumination contained in *The Cantos*? Perhaps a useful predictive statement can be made. What Pound says of his rhetoric is apt and casts light on dark places in the poem. But what Pound claims for the effect of his poem—that it avoids the sins of abstraction and generates new volitions in the reader—must be regarded with some suspicion. But the strongest suspicion must be reserved for Pound's claims to being a social prophet both novel and worthy of credence.

II

As we have seen, the concept at the heart of Pound's thought is that of 'ideas in action'. The exposition of this concept (Essay II) perhaps caused instructed readers to think they were expected to take the concept at Pound's own valuation of it; and doubtless so it should be taken if one is to make much initial headway with the poem. But here the problem is no longer that of perceiving how *The Cantos* responds to its influence; in question now are its supposed uniqueness and its validity.

Though Pound is quite modest in his frequent acknowledgements of his debt to the studies of Fenellosa which introduced the ideogram to him, his estimate of what the ideogram-method will accomplish in poetry and later in our culture is not modest. Acting through *The Cantos*, the 'ideas in action' will assault the modern will effectively —will be the fulcrum to pry the carriage of modern civilization from bad rails to good ones. This—let us concede —is a far from modest estimate of an idea. But if events should justify Pound (and he is optimist enough to expect them to), he would have no reason to be modest. No one pretends that our society does not stand in grim need of renovation. Nor would anyone deny the word epochal to an idea or set of ideas that really 'delivered'—that did for our culture what Pound believes his concept can.

To a point, Pound's development of his central insight into a programme, a basis for action, has a good deal of cogency. We grant that our civilization languishes; we concede that one of the vitiating forces (not the only one) is usury as Pound understands it. As students of literature, we also find it pleasant to agree that it is only the power of language, only the changes it may induce in our modes of thought, that will take us from the evil paths in which we walk. We can see—both from Pound's theory and his practice—that language as it is manipulated now exerts little pressure on our wills and our thoughts. We grant that its custodians have, consciously or unconsciously, sold out to the usurers (or to whatever group or force that, in our judgment, threatens our culture with disunity and decay). It is true that words, for the most part, have come to stand for nothing at all; it is probably true that words must come to stand for something if the society in which we live is to be the expression of something more than clouds of undefined, unsatisfied desires which now surround us.

Pound's vehemence suggests that he is fighting a solitary battle. But there is this large area of agreement that we share with him. Indeed, no one who follows the general movements of Western thought can regard as detached or novel Pound's diagnosis of culture and language disintegration; nor will the observer have to think long to remember the names of other writers who seek to renew a lapsed and betrayed language. (The irresponsibility or the 'treason' of the intellectuals is an old story. It is less often seen that the positive aspect of modern literature struggles to exist. It is composed of new departures— departures that are independent of each other but that nevertheless share two marks. There is a passionate repudiation of the stupidity and venality of the recent literary and political past; novelty is sought out as if the promise of the oracle ran that novelty and experiment will restore tension and strength to the language.)

Therefore, Pound's inferences from the concept, 'ideas in action', must not mislead us. We must make out the 'area of agreement' just sketched. More important—and by that token more difficult to grasp since more is demanded than facile acquiescence to implement this second perception—is it to see that 'ideas in action' is in itself not a novel concept. By framing this concept Pound (whether he wishes to or not) becomes party to a struggle that is not new at all. The struggle is a perennial one, one that is much older than usury itself (at least, as Pound reckons the age of usury).

We are likely to be misled by Pound when we seek to identify this struggle, since (for Pound) the crucial stages of this struggle occur in periods when capitalist-democracy is emerging or dominates. Perhaps to confess that the lineage of the struggle is ancient would be distasteful to Pound, for it would limit the validity of the usurious-nonusurious division that runs through Pound's speculation. But since

that division need not be basic to ours, we damage nothing
dear to us when we perceive that Pound is taking part in
the latest round of the old realist-nominalist struggle: the
struggle that emerged (not for the first time) in history and
embroiled Abelard with Albertus Magnus.

The battle centred on this issue: Have ideas, in some
sense, existence apart from or superior to their temporary
material realization about which sense-impressions inform
us? Or is the only reality which man knows that which
keeps making direct assault on his five senses? The medieval
realists asserted that ideas are superior in being or essence
—without always agreeing on precisely how ideas had won
and maintained this superiority. The nominalists—Abelard
was one of these—insisted that the successive, separate
moments of man's existence were the sources of the only
insights worthy of trust. For the nominalists, ideas—at
least, ideas as their opponents described their existence and
operation—were at best view a deceptive twilight lingering
on after the sun—the sense impressions—had vanished
over the horizon. In another figure, the world as the
nominalist saw it would have slight 'tolerance' for the bur-
dens of abstracted concepts that the other party tried to
make it bear. To respond truthfully and accurately to the
messages which the senses despatch is the whole duty of
man; he misreads his destiny when he fancies, when he
believes, that there are in addition ideas or concepts
curiously self-existent to which he also owes service.

So stated, the twelfth-century battle seems somewhat
arid and devoid of import in a reckoning of Pound's 'ideas
in action' as they do indeed work out in action. How the
old battle went, who won it (Abelard lost) is matter we
expect to encounter in a history of philosophy—matter
we dismiss as representative of the sort of busy work men

invented when (as Pound tirelessly observes) they had nothing *but* words to work with. What must be insisted on, then, is that Pound—all the while he seeks to exploit the benefits of 'ideas in action'—is continuing the ancient nominalist-realist struggle, continuing it on the side of Abelard. That is, he is urging upon a distressed world the curative effects of holding to a nominalist attitude. At least, he is convinced that the first step toward rescuing the world from the clutch of usury lies in discrediting and dispelling the vapid idealism which usury permits to circulate in endowed universities and in the literature it tolerates.

Pound—let us observe immediately—is nowhere so foolish as to assert that idealism (our counterpart of the medieval 'realism' that found concepts in themselves more real than what the senses absorbed *seriatim*) is exclusively the associate of usury. But Pound is sure that it is the climate of idealism that is the climate most favourable to usury; it is insidiously enervating—it discourages men from specific survey and study of the evils of our time. Thus, however grandiose Shelley's ideas, they offer no more than a token resistance to the never-never-land preoccupations of usury: the fantastic and deeply harmful manipulation of credit and rents. Similarly fantastic, indeed, are Shelley's 'progress' and 'humanity'—ideal concepts that harm the usurers not at all, that offer injury to humanity by proffering it, for nourishment, not bread but clouds. Pound notes several times that medieval 'realism' was, as an intellectual construct, vastly superior to modern idealistic systems that keep us from having a precise view of our culture. True, the medieval systems Pound reprehends may have no closer touch with the five senses than their present counterpart; but the systems of Aquinas and others can at least provide esthetic pleasure, for the scholastics were able to manipulate their needlessly multiplied entities with grace and precision: both virtues of presentation that usury would rather not encounter, even in the realm of self-existent ideas.

But, praise the medieval 'realists' as one will, one must not ever forget that they sponsored habits of thought that detached men from the life of the five senses, the nominalist reality. Abelard's resistance to these habits necessitated a work of destruction to precede the work of construction; he—or any other foe of 'realism' ancient or modern—would have to discredit 'realist' approaches to crucial problems before he would have any chance of displaying the profits inhering in his way of approach. In exactly the same way, Pound sees his labours beginning with a struggle to discredit the debased, shoddy version of 'realism' that usury permits in our culture. Pound must win this battle (by explicit prose argument, by use of the method of the ideogram that is the basis of *The Cantos*) before he can really point to the profit of depending on his version of nominalism, of discovering counsel and motive force in 'ideas in action.' If we recall what this concept really comes to, we see that it is sheerly nominalist. For the concept is a distillation of Pound's reading of human experience. Special events in human history and special facets of past human culture remain potentially sovereign for our current ills so long as our handling of history and past culture allows the import of a special event to remain firmly attached to the moment in time at which it first occured. The special event must be kept firmly localized, crusted over with all in the way of the peculiar and the grotesque that being localized offers as opposition to the facile operations of a generalizing or abstracting 'realism'.

In Pound's language, whenever we abstract an 'idea' from
an 'idea in action', we really abstract the non-existent from
the richly existing; worse, we dissolve the precious entity
that a specific event, an 'idea in action', once was. If nothing
worse, we play an intellectual game when we pretend that
the good, the true, and the beautiful have any sort of independent existence, even as objects of thought. Pound
would say that the good person, the true saying, and the
arresting act have indeed an existence that can be reconstructed for us, either by study or the practice of poetry.
But both student and poet must be content to allow the
reconstructed person, saying, or act to remain half-hidden,
even disfigured; it must continue to lurk in the integument
of contingency by which it was hemmed in when it made
its first, last, and only direct assault on the five senses. At
the time of emergence, it had power to move, to signify.
Art that tries—as Pound's does—to recreate that power
must mimic not only the event or deed but also all that
hemmed it in. All the aspects of the moment of emergence,
of existence, must be suggested and not—the sin of
'idealizing' art—only selected aspects. All past events
partake of the nature of Antaeus; they have strength to
instruct us so long as they are in touch with their mother,
the earth. We must be willing to cherish the specific
moment which we strive to reconstruct *as it was*; we must
not permit it to be altered by cloudy conceptions of what
it ought to have been 'ideally'.

This battle of Pound's, however individualized by his
statement of the grounds on which it may properly be
fought, should be seen as part of a general struggle that
animates Western culture at present—or convulses it. Let
us not be misled by Pound's own account, an account which
always suggests that he fights alone—alone not merely

because he lacks companions but alone because he is not even comprehended. Comprehension of Pound's poetry, of his 'gestures', has indeed been faulty; but one need not go on and grant that what he has tried to do lacks parallels. What we must see is that Pound's cries and assertions, Pound's poetry, are not absolutely *sui generis*; we must not let the bravado of Pound's claims determine our estimate of them.

We have placed Pound's struggle in the region of ideas (if such a region may be mentioned in discussion of a person who denies that such a region exists). It is necessary here to suggest that a capital aspect of the 'crisis' of our culture is the continuation, in our culture, of the realist-nominalist struggle. In our days, the stuggle is fought, naturally, not with medieval weapons but with the instruments we chance on in contemporary armories. There is no lack of weapons in these arsenals; they are stocked full, thanks to the impressive advances of modern science, thanks to the less impressive ins and outs of the intellectual history of the past three centuries. We need to see in what precise ways Pound's 'ideas in action' employ weapons quite familiar to us—a way that is not entirely unfamiliar either. When we rehearse, as here, what the 'ideas in action' are—words and acts resolutely undifferentiated from the contingent, condemned to wither the instant they are detached from the moment—we should hear familiar chimes ringing.

Familiar because, as the constrictions of our time increase, the sorties and counter-sorties tend to repeat, in 'modern dress', the opposition of Abelard and Albertus Magnus. To refer to a struggle on the stage of American education is perhaps to bring in evidence that Pound would regard as beneath notice. Nevertheless, the division between teachers who regard education as being chiefly an exposure to immediate experience and those who feel that education should bring the student into contact with experience as it has been studied and perhaps codified by the wise of other ages—all this is a kind of nominalist-realist division. One party to the struggle says, 'Only life itself can instruct', and the other group says, 'Only that which has been extracted from life—only that which is permanent in the ebb and flow of life—can instruct'.

Some readers will doubt, at this point, that one illustrates a crisis in Western culture—a crisis in which Pound and his poem participate—by referring to a matter that is literally academic and perhaps figuratively so. If so, substitute for this illustration other nominalist-realist cleavages. Consider, for example, the gulf that divides the masters of jurisprudence who, by hypothesis, believe in the existence of a natural law, a 'real' entity, a *jus gentium* that is binding upon all persons, whatever their nationality or religion (the Nuremburg trials presuppose the existence of such a law) and the no less positive propagandists who refuse to bind themselves or the state they serve by any tyrannical entities: the good of their state consists in the satisfaction of a current pressing need. The state, thus nominalistically conceived, is from one moment to the next, its own master, its own guide to future goals. It cannot be asked to submit to restrictions upon its activity suggested by a religious or juristic non-entity called 'the conscience of mankind'. Even on the level of personal behaviour we cannot be unaware of the clash between persons who 'realistically' insist on observance of certain fixed, supposedly permanent standards of behaviour and those who judge that each moment, each situation, exists to give us an essential clue to action—a clue (in theory, at any rate) quite unlike hints that other moments have given us. Would not these latter persons find congenial Pound's insistence that we cultivate the only garden that we can really hope to cultivate: the immediate one that the five senses make available to us, where 'ideas in action' can send down deep tap-roots, tap-roots that we must not dream of cutting—at least, if we prefer live flowers to a herbarium in which are found lifeless plants from which moisture and pungency are gone?

This list of familiar examples should suffice to support the contention that Pound is involved in a conflict deeper than fascist-democratic, a battle that in the last few generations has been fought not across boundaries but inside the boundaries of all the nations of which we have much knowledge. What must be condemned or accepted is not Pound the fascist (a word that tends to lose its precise significance now that it is applied to anything one happens to dislike); it is Pound the nominalist (as a thinker, as a poem) that we must approve or censure. He is essentially one of a company that locates truth and wisdom in the transient moment; he—like many other persons (many of them highly respected)—denies that truth exists in a fashion different from that in which the moment exists. In other words, the crux of the Pound problem is neither a political or economic one, though—as we have seen— the problem seems to be stated in political and economic terms. The crux is, rather, this one: in what fashion do we read from experience; in what ways are we to lead others to read experience as we have read it? The poet is a political animal; yes. But he is a political animal not concerned with politics in any narrow sense—concerned rather with understanding and 'rendering' the inclusive view that alone makes 'politics' bearable. Pound would say that 'politics' are bearable only when discussed and manipulated nominalistically, only when brought into contact with 'ideas in action'. This faith of Pound's—shall we call it the deification of the realized moment?—generates certain problems, in and out of poetry. (The opposite faith—faith that concepts have an existence to some degree independent of the successions of moments—generates *its* problems, problems that do not concern us in this essay.) The problem—political, it will be seen—is this: how, from a perception of moments, of particles of reality, can there emerge a really altered sensitivity, a will whose reorientation can be termed both 'better' and permanent? To make a brutal stricture, is this not to expect from the impact of the 'ideas in action' the very results that 'realists' (medieval and modern) used quite emptily to believe came from assiduous exposure of the mind to the proper set of abstract ideas?

Pound, at any rate, is confident that the discipline of *The Cantos*, of the method of the ideogram, will re-found sensitivities; and it will make them harmonious and strong without any nonsensical talk about harmony and strength. It is the duty of a teacher of gymnastics to cultivate 'form'; but he usually does so without much talk about form. Indeed, talk *about* form would doubtless confuse the minds attached to the splendid bodies in the teacher's charge. The body—and, with Pound, the will—is instructed by doing. This parallel, though close, is unjust to Pound at one point. He is a nominalist, he believes that the will must be assaulted by 'engines' forged in a nominalist workshop; but he is not the ordinary sort of anti-intellectualist. A fair judge must concede that he uses his own mind rigorously; and it is plain that he expects his readers to respond keenly and accurately to the stimuli he offers them in *The Cantos*. In what other way can the general reorientation of the will be effected?

However, the fact remains that salvation by immediate experience is indeed the opposite of salvation by shared and perhaps imposed concepts. Further, one must grant that a trust in 'ideas in action' pervades many quarters of modern literature. (An artist who uses language can avoid the entire problem only by working so minutely that what concerns Pound cannot come into play.) How else explain the almost mystical attachment to presentation of the thing-in-itself which informs a good deal of literary realism or naturalism? It cannot escape an observer that the naturalistic writer, after denying that his work stands in any relation to 'first principles', makes a leech-level survey of his slice of life—almost as if he hoped that the significance he denied elsewhere will emerge here. More interesting revolts than that of naturalism against the tyranny of conceptualism in art are Joyce's *Ulysses* and *Finnegans Wake*. It is as if (for Joyce) each moment, waking or dreaming, holds all the meaning of experience, even though—perhaps 'because' —it is quite independent of all other moments. This being true, the artist does well to exercise all his ingenuity as he stalks each separate moment, each 'idea in action'. Moreover, each stalking would be a new one, nor would one's present stalking be much aided by what one has learned from other intense forays on the moment in itself. Nominalism *à outrance* would seem to produce, on the literary stage, such an approach. Careless readers of *The Cantos* might think these remarks describe what one finds in Pound's poem; they do not, for reasons that will soon be clear. There is more in *The Cantos* than devout prostration before the object, the moment without filiations. Devout prostration is, I suppose, a non-political attitude.

Pound's treatment of the moment, the only really

numinous object in human experience, is qualified by the intensity, the protractedness, of the struggle in which he senses he is immersed. Before the moment can be adored, ideas in the form of general statements or coercive procedures must be driven from our culture. For Pound, this is the step which 'costs'—costs in effort, in ingenuity, in courtship of failure even. Involved in taking this, Pound cannot take one that would otherwise be highly attractive to him: that of maintaining that each moment is utterly detached, utterly devoid of correspondences with other moments. This latter step is an easy one to take; it leads the artist to a series of fervent embraces that can have no consequences, can lead to no entanglements. Furthermore, faith in the uniqueness of each moment forbids one from comparing embraces. Yet Pound, as a political animal, is committed to comparing embraces, to expecting consequences from them. He is intellectually a fervid endorser of the nominalist point of view; but he also hopes fervently for 'results'. On what basis may a nominalist work for results? Can he so work without diminishing the gulf that he wants to keep between himself and all forms of conceptualism?

French painters, recall, did not choose to remain at the point reached by Monet, a satisfaction with the endless and varying parades of light across the dissolving planes of a cathedral. They sought, rather, to organize the impressions which Monet had made available to them; and what they chiefly knew was that the organization they sought in their paintings could not be in accordance with traditional artistic canons. Pound too seeks to organize the moments, the separate sensations which study and experience have given him. But he must do this without falling back on abstract ideas. So he enters on a path fraught with troubles at every turn. For this is the dilemma imposed on Pound by his faith: abstract ideas have time and again betrayed man; moments utterly separate—however real, however intense—cannot guide man. Pound, evangelist that he is, wants to guide man without betraying him. The 'purity' of Pound's artistic development is hampered by his desire to gratify an ambition that is complex—that is (some would say) impossible of realization.

What Pound tries to do is clarified if we remember the solution of the problem arrived at by certain semanticists. These students of communication start, usually, from some sort of nominalist position. Though anti-Aristotelian, they have no desire (Pound has no desire) to reduce communication to an abstract algebra of successive moments or predications. (Carnap seems to travel toward this last-mentioned goal.) Instead, successive moments must preserve a content of human import without—shall we say—getting that content frozen, without falling into the rigidities that afflict idealistic systems. The human import of each moment must be kept *un*frozen, palpitant; and yet that import must somehow—here is the miracle asked for—establish relation with other imports equally unique and separate. How is this to be done?

By a process, certain semanticists say, which can be called 'time-binding'. Time-binding differs—that it really does differ depends on an act of faith and cannot be supported by clear experiment—from the process of abstraction in that the person who is time-binding is able to put into one bouquet flowers culled from various gardens *without* causing the flowers which make up the bouquet to lose their separate beauty and aroma. (They do lose this beauty and aroma when they are rudely gathered and 'pressed' by a seeker after clear ideas.)

Here one is tempted to ask a question. Does not the
time-binder's culling of the living flowers after all cut
their tap-roots and take them away from the morsel of
earth where each flower had its only proper existence?
The practicers of time-binding maintain that what they do
is quite unlike the process of abstraction. They enjoy—it
is not quite clear how—all the advantages of inducing
'generals' without exposing their processes of thought to
any of the vitiating dangers that dog conceptual thinking,
such as lack of touch with immediate reality or humiliating
subservience to 'compounded' concepts incorrectly put
together by ancient dogmatists.

Perhaps the implicit counsel of certain semanticists is
that we should not shed tears for the demise of man 'the
rational animal'. For in their eyes, man is still set aside from
the rest of brute creation because he is the 'time-binding'
animal: an animal (if not perverted by bad training) that
can cull guidance from his multifarious experience without
causing any particle of that experience to lose its sovereignty
of impact, the immediacy to which (we have noted) is
attached a mystical significance scarcely less intense than
that once discovered in 'the One'. Time-binding (some of
its defenders might even grant) is perhaps very close to
the process of abstracting, but abstracting with all the
marks of original intellectual sin removed: the sin that
tempts us to think that reality exists otherwhere than at the
ends of the nerves that serve the five senses, the sin that
makes us suppose that man's final dignity lies in thought
rather than in sensation. It is plain that 'right' time-binding
is chiefly a question of 'right' sensation. Questions of logic,
of mental processes, may indeed enter in; but they are to
be minimized since they can be regarded as the automatic
meshing of gears subsequent to the pressing of the right

buttons—that is, the accurate collection of material presented by the five senses.

The Cantos, it seems to me, is the product of a sustained attempt to present—in practice rather than by general description—an actual experiment in time-binding. We have seen that, for Pound, the necessity to act, to will, to reshape an evil world, makes the rapt adoration of the separate moment neither defensible nor tolerable. Here, indeed, is the underlying reason for Pound's detaching himself from the early imagist 'programme'; for that 'programme' did indeed advocate prostrating oneself before the moment, the object-in-itself—one would cherish, as superior to such impure, practical activities as time-binding, the tracing of the lineaments of the instant. Is not this conflict relative to the proper treatment of what experience, from instant to instant, presents the old conflict between Martha and Mary? Mary sits at the feet of the Lord, the supreme and unique instant, and practices adoration; and Martha works to get the meal on the table. Pound, in mid-career, came to the conclusion that his lot (as a poet) was the task of getting the meal on the table: something that had not been done properly for generations. His was the labour of readying and directing a wide world of the imagination that would serve as a basis for future practical action.

But if Pound chose the activity of Martha, it had to be that activity on terms that do not vitiate such activity; there must be no contact with general concepts, with herbarium ideas. So the path of Pound (in *The Cantos*) is beset with dangers, just as—also of necessity—the path of his readers is beset with obscurities that cannot be removed. For the obscurities are the token that Pound remains on guard against the idealist incursions that would

EZRA POUND AND *THE CANTOS*

enervate both the writing and the reading of *The Cantos*.

It helps us—wrestling at this point as we do with time-binding, with the ideogram—to look for a moment at the history of modern painting. French impressionism, it can be argued, is the equivalent, in painting, of imagism in American poetry. Both represent extreme, almost mystical nominalist poses. The poet before the moment, Monet from hour to hour before his cathedral or his haystack where form and identity dissolved in the interplay of light and colour—these two experiences are not unlike. And while there is no 'movement' called 'post-imagism' —*post*, that is, the attitude in poetry that pushes the nominalist dogma to an extreme point, the effort that produced *The Cantos* resembles the section of art history called post-impressionism. The only unity that section of art history displays is that all the efforts it comprehends are alike in that they express perceptions of the futility of dreaming to prolong the achievements of Sisley, Monet, *et al*. Post-impressionist effort seeks—to use the term the semanticists have given us—some sort of time-binding: time-binding, however, that will not plunge art back into (say) the inanities of David and Ingres, into what (in art) can be regarded as the equivalent of conceptualism. Any study of post-impressionism is likely to see cubism and other 'movements' as having in common a point of departure (if little else): a point of departure—consider the role of imagism in Pound's development—not bad in itself but, with certain goals in mind, too limited. Similarly, for painting that wants to move, to develop, even to arrive, impressionism (the absorption of the artist, his tools, his technique into the thing, the thing momentary and the thing mystical) reaches a limit; it appears that there is nothing more to be done with nature in itself than what

Monet has done. What can be done instead? Nature can—
to mention various 'programmes'—be worked over in
terms of the cube, the subconscious, the dream. (I lump
together matters that in other contexts would deserve the
sharpest dissociation.) The artist must resist being absorbed
into the great display of radiance and colour-vibration
which is nature; he must seek to perform—for nature and
even in despite of nature—an act of time-binding, of culling
and grouping its flowers without (the crux for Pound as
well as for modern painting) causing them to wither.

We can see that post-impressionism has at least resisted
falling back into the artistic sins that correspond to the
intellectual sin of abstraction: the sin, for example, of
Poussin in whose paintings landscapes, human bodies,
and even ruins are idealized (if we can trust our taste) to
the point of nullity. Was it not Cezanne's desire 'to do over
Poussin according to nature'? Did he not wish to group
and regulate the observations that the impressionists had
justly drawn from nature, observations 'right' as far as
they went but not enough? From nature itself—rather
than from a set of academic principles—must be drawn an
order of perception, of arrangement, that would not dena-
ture nature as Poussin had.

All such modern attempts at order and arrangement—
Cezanne's to Picasso's—are (in comparison to what Pound
attempts in *The Cantos*) comparatively easy of achievement.
They are comparatively easy simply because of the medium
involved (colour and line and the 'vibrations' the two can
set up). Identical effects are, we shall soon see, impossible
of achievement in the medium of words and rhythm.
Specifically, Cezanne was not—as he 'time-bound'—in
danger of falling into the inanities of Poussin, of having
much 'truck' with the 'idea' or the Ideal. And however

EZRA POUND AND *THE CANTOS*

eccentric other post-impressionist time-binding (principle may follow principle notoriously, as in the career of Picasso), we are in no danger of seeing in Picasso's *Guernica* or Chirico's early perspectives a pernicious return to earlier artistic practice when art was hag-ridden by the Ideal.

In painting, then, meaning or concepts are secondary. (That does not mean 'unimportant'.) But with written expression, 'meaning' is or tends to become primary. Whatever present theories of poetry may say, words do not have the detachability from context, from the history of their use in the past, that colour and line have. Perhaps for those who still seek 'purity', a terminus exists: the study of higher mathematics. And perhaps one may even, for painting and music, tolerate such a definition of art as this: Art tends to the conditions of mathematics. One may tolerate the definition, provided one understands that the verb *tends* signalizes an inclination that will not be realized. But the definition is hardly one that casts much light on what literature is; and I say this with unorthodox recent developments in mind. Further, I underline this reservation to suggest that the parallel we have drawn between post-impressionism and 'post-imagism' as it works out in *The Cantos* was intended to remind us of what the nominalist dilemma is; it was not intended to predict our judgment of the time-binding efforts of Pound's poem. That is, Cezanne may do over Poussin according to nature, and we may be quite willing to concede that he has done something that fulfils his promise, that he has done justice to nature without repeating the idealistic sins of Poussin. We may concede still more—that he has turned from the utter nominalism of Monet without becoming a returned votary at the shrine of the Ideal.

What we have now to ask is whether Pound's retreat from utter nominalism (which is, humanly speaking, quite as productive of inanity as the exact opposite, utter devotion to the undifferentiated One) has been as successful as Cezanne's and others. If it is successful, we should expect to find these two things: first, the creation of a sufficiently directing form, the literary analogue of the slopes of Mont Ste. Victoire; second—and here we bow to Pound's professed programme—exertion of sufficient pressure on the human will to produce a reorientation free of the dangers of idealism or abstractions: an aim, I feel, that is not open to one who works in colour and line rather than in words.

The answer to the first question—whether there is, in *The Cantos*, a sufficiently directing form, will have to remain a subjective one. But as for the second point—whether Pound's poem works on the will as he hopes it will work —I think it will be possible to be quite objective.

Perhaps the answer to the first question may take this form. We are aware that (in our present terms) a time-binding process is at all points under weigh in *The Cantos*. We are aware of cross-references, of clusters of ideograms that (like bees swarming) mysteriously but demonstrably swarm together. We have already seen, in an earlier essay, that each cluster of ideograms gets *some* of its cohesion because of its polarity to another cluster. How keenly this cohesion, this polarity, is felt must remain a matter for individual judgment.

But to answer the second query—whether Pound's poem actually makes the impact on the will that he desiderates —we can suggest a fairly objective answer. But we must commence by parcelling up this question, as follows. If the poem exercises coercion on the will, is that coercion effectively explained in nominalistic terms or in terms quite opposite? Does the coercion, if we grant it is in some way exerted, avoid the dangers said to inhere in the activity of professed idealism—such dangers as over-simplification of a problem and delusive separation from the complex reality that is man's only true reality, moment-to-moment experience? If it does not avoid these dangers, what is it that catches up with *The Cantos*: a defect in the poet, or factors of frustration in language itself? In brief, what is the real effect of *The Cantos*—the one Pound confidently predicts or some other?

The coercion, one may begin by saying, is *not* effected along purely nominalistic lines. It is not even effected along the relatively nominalistic lines that (we have just seen) provide many a post-impressionist painter some basis for operation. Why is it that what is admittedly a delicate adjustment in painting becomes quite impossible for Pound? Why does the time-binding in *The Cantos* actually come so much nearer the 'sins' of abstraction? The answer is this. The artist who works in line and colour has a free field for his experiments once he has shattered (as many a painter and his critical sponsors have indeed been able to shatter) the public's habitual expectations as to painting: that pictures have a subject, that they should correspond to what our defective vision reports of reality. To shatter these habitual expectations was not easy (*vide* the critical battles fought over the successive efforts to present, on canvas, a new arrangement); but they have, by now, among the cognoscenti and the semi-cognoscenti, been shattered. The result is that to-day the knowing approach a new painter or a new 'period' of an old artist with no expectations whatever except a hope to discover novelty, to see how this time nature has been rearranged. Perhaps the only objective test now applied to a new picture is whether there is—to a special rearrangement—an inner cohesion, a 'go' that the cultivated sensibility may respond to. If this is so in art, why is it not possible in literature? Why may we not become accustomed there to the destruction of old expectations, the creation of new sets of attention? Pound plainly has faith that such a destruction and creation are quite possible.

There is an important difference that this analogy between painting and poetry must not conceal, a simple but a crucial one. Pound, as artist, submits to the bondage not of line and colour but to the bondage of words: a much more onerous bondage. Line and colour appeal direct to the sense of sight; and it is fairly easy to detach the sense of sight from the earlier expectations to which it has been —some would say 'badly'—habituated. Thus, the 'bondage' exercised by past use of line and colour really rests lightly on the shoulders of the painter. (Whether this is so in music, still less a representative art—whether a public's expectations of rhythm, melody, and tonality can be so easily reshaped —I leave undecided. Perhaps the expectations which we bring to music, though not related to representation, may have roots deeper and more ineradicable than those possessed by line and colour.) Words also are, in their way, ineradicable. Their roots are their rhythms, their long-established harmonies with each other, their traditional ways of coming into relation with each other (and I mean more than grammar and syntax here). So the question reshapes itself thus for *The Cantos*. Can nature be rearranged in the medium of language, of an established verbal vehicle, without—so intractable is this medium, so habitual its evolutions once they are set in motion—a reproduction of some of the effects judged (by Pound and others) to be pernicious? I do not think so.

Pound would, I am sure (as would a great many other writers who apply their talents to similar tasks) deny this with all the considerable vehemence at his command. He would maintain that *his* attack on the reader's sensibility, that the entire educative impact of *The Cantos*, reshapes the habitual patterns of our language, redirects its evolutions, arouses new expectations and then satisfies them. There are (he would argue) no abstractions or abstracting in *The Cantos*; rather is there a series of pure sensations, poignant and intense. It is because of lengthy submission to these sensations that the reader rises a changed person, his will urging him to travel in a new direction, his mind purified of those modes of employing words that have been the bane of Western capitalist-democratic culture. We may be willing to grant—as we have done—that a comparable reversal of will and sensibility may well take place in persons responsive to the full effects of (say) Picasso's reorganizations in line and colour. But that such a reversal follows upon a careful reading of *The Cantos* is a hope rather than a fact. Such is the compulsion—some will say, 'Such is the tyranny'—inherent in our language. We are not, of course, prohibited from depicting for ourselves the results of the cessation of the law of gravity, a shift in the condensing point of vapour. But only the writers of 'science fiction' try to follow out fancies about altered laws of nature; and we must observe that Pound comes close to realizing his myth of an altered language very seldom. What he does in *The Cantos* is different from what he judges he is doing. This observation does not deny merit to the poem; it seeks rather to clarify the merit that the poem really has.

What follows—as 'proof' of the observations just made, as clarification of Pound's poem—is, naturally, the product of one person's reading of *The Cantos*. It is possible that other sensibilities will give a different response to the poem. It is possible, that is, that the poem will indeed re-educate other wills without creating, in the process, abstractions perfectly recognizable, perfectly discutible. But until that happens—until, for a large body of readers, Pound's myth of language-as-it-ought-to-be coincides with the effects of language encountered in the actual poem—the following may perhaps be accepted as an account of what 'happens' to a mind in contact with *The Cantos*. It is an account of being involved not only in time-binding but in abstractions; for, despite the embarrassments which Pound provides, language manages to behave in its wonted fashion —within the limits provided by the English language, at least. For that matter, one should remain sceptical that Chinese is as free from the evil process of abstracting as Pound supposes. The 'machinery' of that language may not happen to produce words and locutions as obviously removed from sense-experience as ours. But that is no indication that the human mind will not be up to its old *in*carnalities, even in Chinese. Such an assertion amounts to widening the argument, to saying that Pound strives against the structure of man's mind itself. There is a good deal of evidence that the human mind, beginning though it does with sense, cannot be restrained from hobbling on determinedly towards the abstractions that it usually manages badly, that it is very often deceived by. It is not irrelevant to note here what Chinese tell us about names like Cherry Blossom and Precious Wind, names that seem to us delicate and poetic and concrete. Such names arouse, in the Chinese breast, no more emotion than that which *we* feel when we hear a girl called Violet or Opal. In either language, any sensed metaphor has long since evaporated; both Precious Wind and Violet function as characterless tags—as, in a sense, words abstracted from concrete uses. So, one may suspect, with other elements in a language that, to Pound's taste, has a richness of sensual compulsion that English lacks. In any language, then—to take a dark view—the human mind staggers drunkenly after the potations that betray it. It does not cease systematizing impressions vivid and momentary. It is—in an earlier figure—not content with culling flowers only; it must press them. The intended effect of *The Cantos* may be to present the reader a bouquet that shall magically redirect our wills without taking us through a preliminary intellectual act of understanding, botanizing, what the poem dispersedly presents.

The effect of the poem—the question of the *intended* effect to one side—is this: the succession of special impacts, of ideogram blocks, gives rise to a set of general statements—statements quite comprehensible and not at all recherchés. These general statements become the object—as does any general statement—of the process of analysis and judgment (acceptance or rejection) which is our 'response' to any sort of over-arching or inclusive meaning. This is not to deny that the will, the emotions, do give the immediate vibration to many a vivid image in the poem; it is to deny that will, after being stirred, moves immediately toward the sort of functioning that Pound expects of it. We may be able to suppress a deviation into intellectual analysis when we look at Picasso's *Guernica*; but we cannot during the good many hours that *The Cantos* demand of us. Nor is this 'failure' of ours *vis à vis The Cantos* our fault. Let us put the matter at its simplest, ignoring questions about what the psyche common to humanity may be. Mr. Pound and we, his readers, share a language. So long as he and we move within the confines of that language, we must submit to *its* coercion as well as to that of the ideogram. It is simply impossible to stop at the point where Pound would want us to stop, the point beyond which permissible and necessary time-binding degenerates into abstract thinking—even though we are aware of Pound's unclear caveat, 'Thus far and no farther'. We concede that Pound is no enemy of certain sorts of general statement, as many a passage in *Culture* shows. We know that what he really wishes to do is to discredit certain specific abstractions, bad abstractions that bully and stupify mankind. To whatever degree we sympathize, we cannot keep from noting that what the poet of *The Cantos* really strives for is not to tear out all abstractions (his expressed programme) but to tear out of the mind and the will the evil abstractions and to implant there concepts no less generalized, even though they are approached obliquely by means of the ideogram. These beneficial concepts are seldom directly referred to in the poem; that is unnecessary since their presence is pervasive. The mode of their existence is indeed somewhat novel, but that must not deceive us as to what they are; they are concepts, and it is special pleading to ask that, because their existence has been 'coerced' in the mind of the reader rather than explicitly conferred on them by the poet, they should receive, at our hands, treatment different from that which we allot to other concepts that we encounter more directly and simply. The end-product of the method of the ideogram is not different in kind from the end-products of poets who handle language in a way that does not confuse us at all. This is not to say that the technique of *The Cantos* is a mistaken or wasted one; we have, in an earlier section, surveyed the grounds on which one can claim that the 'devices' of *The Cantos* are worthy of the sharpest attention, for technically *The Cantos* is both ingenious and sound. But the perception we must hold to here is that ingenuity and soundness of technique are no warrant that the general ideas to which the poem ministers are either ingenious (that is, arrived at in ways other than that by which we compound, from available examples, any idea) or sound (that is, frames of reference which can enrich our comprehension of the crisis in Western culture).

The concepts which are created in our minds by a reading of *The Cantos* constitute two or three brief statements about civilization. Man has a large range of feeling which the relatively good society—Pound has no illusions about discovering or creating a society absolutely good—allows expression; a relatively bad society stifles the expression of the range of feeling. The problem of the immediate future is to undermine and destroy the economic order that supports usury, to set up an order which—like Italian Fascism as Pound saw it—will inhibit full expression of emotions and talents as little as possible.

This set of ideas is what Pound's poem is 'about'. Since the poem urges on us participation in political and social action, since the approach proper to 'pure' poetry is irrelevant, we should not hesitate to complete our analysis of Pound's concepts *as* concepts instead of offering up deep but mindless stirrings of the will which Pound chiefly wishes to produce by his poem.

We need not hesitate, then, to recognize—in Pound's ideas, in the relation to them of the ideogram blocks in his poem—the sort of over-simplification or, even, detachment from reality that Pound himself—and justly—perceives in the glosses nineteenth century poetry provided for the world. Indeed, the sins of over-simplification, of detachment from complexity, which we can observe in *The Cantos* or in the concepts it 'coerces' us to form are just as sinful as the blemishes which Pound objects to in gross idealism. Pound, to be sure, would insist on this distinction: the professed idealist's balloon is bound to earth by no more than three or four cords (concepts from which everything else in a system is inferred); whereas, there are innumerable cords binding Pound's concepts to earth. If time-binding is a fair term for describing Pound's substitute for conventional methods of abstracting, then the cords binding Pound's concepts to the earth are quite beyond numbering. For time-binding, we are told, differs from abstracting in that each concept is linked with one sensory experience and one only. True, it may closely resemble other concepts similarly tethered; but a person who binds time never goes on to commit the idealistic sin of constituting an intellectual entity from concepts that resemble each other.

If it is true then that in the mind each valid concept is linked to only one percept, Pound's trouble in *The Cantos* is that the ropes get badly snarled; there is, in other terms, at least an effect of abstraction and rather naive abstraction at that. What makes for this confusion? What makes *The Cantos* a less subtle poem than it ought, in some lights, to be? The answer is—Pound's guiding passions—his enmity to a certain economic system; his devotion (by now secondary) to certain human powers. This latter passion, the devotion to the 'human', operates in the poem in an undiscriminating way. Pound would have no patience with the reader who preferred the concept that is linked with the 'idea in action' that is John Adams to the concept connected with Malatesta. Both men are anti-usuristic. Is that not enough?

Enough, certainly, to reduce the real complexity of historical and present-day experience to a simple opposition that corresponds less to reality than to the rich contents of Pound's mind as he broods on reality, as he shapes his poem. Ironically, the trouble with the ideas that organize the poem, that are served by the method of the ideogram, is that they are too general; they tend to make the tension of the poem as much a matter of black-and-white opposition as that of heaven to hell-mouth in medieval drama. Consequently, the experience of good and evil that *The Cantos* forces upon our wills is one that we are constantly tempted to check or correct by our own fairly complex experience of social and cultural forms. The poem offers us an experience of good and evil inferior, for example, to experiences open to the reader of Dostoyevsky, where the opposition of the two forces exists even more strongly, but where brash schematization (by either author or reader) is difficult since the novels show at every turn how intimately the two forces interpenetrate in human experience. It is Pound's failure to do justice to the fact of interpenetration, of gradation, that creates (beneath the complex surface of his poem) an underlying effect of naiveté. (One thinks, in this connection, of that other Russian, Tolstoy, whose most painstakingly prepared novel, *Resurrection*, fails to convince because of the flat suppositions that dominated the writer as he worked out his story of prison life. If there is such an impulse as the treatise-writing impulse, its workings can be observed in both Tolstoy and Pound.)

Pound's naiveté consists in taking a partial explanation —in many ways, a truthful one—for a complete explanation. No one can doubt that usury has contributed greatly to the inhumanity of the era in which we live; there are strong reasons for doubting that it is the only begetter of the evil which we know. We must draw back from sharing Pound's hope in its ultimate simplicity: that with the destruction of usury, we destroy the virus that is solely responsible for our sickness. There is, we suspect, much more that will have to be destroyed, nor will it be so easy to name and come at. And though we cannot doubt that a purification of language will contribute to the reconstruction of our society, we cannot hope that it will effect that reconstruction. Reconstruction, as understood by Pound, is almost exclusively a process of removing fetters, of freeing human beings from an enchanter's spell. In legend, once the spell is broken, the story is at an end; we have strong reasons for believing that, even with usury overthrown, our story would but be at a beginning. Pound, at this point, shows for a kind of Quietist, waiting for the descent of the Holy Spirit, expecting the painless emergence of a rich humanity in which we all shall share. Study of history suggests that the emergence of a full humanity in any period was a painful one, subject to chance, subject to the absence or presence of a variety of factors—certainly not made possible by the non-existence of one factor alone: usury.

But Pound, we know, is an indefatigable student of cultural history. But those studies—and *The Cantos*—have been invigorated by hatred rather than hope. Pound's hopes for humanity are various and not easily distinguished from each other. Only Pound's hatred is single; and it is as simplifying of reality as is the central tenet of a radically idealistic system. It is the power of the evil he attacks that gives Pound's poem focus. The 'goods' that concern him are pluralistically conceived; it is a rank idealistic sin, in Pound's eyes, to try to relate one good to another. Thus, in his presentation of the good, the human objects and deeds, Pound suffers the fate that has dogged other pluralists; expression of widely scattered affections can never suggest a devotion that is either directed or intense. It is as a Monist—or, better, as a Manichean who is out of touch with the beings of light but is still in close contact with the powers of darkness—that Pound is effective. He is an indiscriminate commender of excellence; but his palate for evil knows, for certain vintages, what it is about.

A defender of Pound *in toto* might suggest that the poet of *The Cantos* does not pretend to be more than the leader of a section-crew that is making clear the track, that is removing the wreckage left on it by the nineteenth century and ours. Should one demand more? A little. There are, one might say, different ways of clearing wreckage from tracks. The single hate, the single ascription to capitalist-democracy of all our present evil, may prolong the delay of repairing past damage. It may, poetically speaking, keep the writer from rendering correctly the 'idea in action'; he may, that is, finally prove inadequate to the single moment which *The Cantos* must present justly—fail because of the simplicity of vision we have just noted. And if the poet does not render the 'idea in action' correctly, what chance is there that he will get far in the task of clearing the right of way?

Finally, cautious introspection presents to all of us the knowledge that no single moment, no 'idea in action', really exists in itself, out of contact with vividly remembered moments. Nor does Pound deny this except when he gives conscious expression to the nominalist tendency bred in him by his revolt against hypocritical idealism or (worse) the verbal self-hypnosis of some poets. One does not need to say—with an accent of medieval 'realism'—that man is the rational animal. If one says merely that man is a time-binding animal (perhaps a distinction without a difference), one says in effect that man is the animal that compares, that has the habit of ranking things according to the presence or absence of pleasure or intensity. So will any reader of *The Cantos* continue to approach the ideograms. Such procedure Pound in some moods would repudiate as a left-hand approach to idealism. It is as if his credo would run: man should hate usury and love a multitude of goods without inhibiting the spontaneous movements of the will by the acts of judging and arranging.

It is this hope, central to Pound's thought and his poem, the hope that modern man can be made so to hate and love, that we must regard as unrealistic. Our sensibilities, 'conditioned' by unreflective life in a usurious world, are doubtless corrupt. But we find in ourselves and historical record a greater variety of hates than Pound reveals. Further, we find that mankind—from hope of survival as well as to gratify a thirst for systematizing—has always submitted (as well as to the compulsion of the irreducible moment) to a need for arranging (in order of intensity, or pleasure, or survival value) the good and evil which he perceives in successive moments.

By saying this, we do not fall into the simplification, the abstraction, which we can perceive in Pound's presentation of evil. (Pound, the pluralist collector of 'goods', is 'righter' than Pound, the monistic hater of usury—'righter', but less effective.) We continue, rather, to be aware that men are just as curious about the interrelations of good and evil, of good and good, of evil and evil, as they are about the possible division between good and evil which is the intellectual capital on which Pound's poem draws. This continuing curiosity is as much a 'fact' about mankind as each moment in itself, each 'idea in action'. It is a fact that Pound ignores, a taste that his poem is not designed to satisfy. His neglect is natural; complex, involved curiosity never sorts well with prophetic fervour, whether the fervour be Jeremiah's or Ezra Pound's. Yet this is the very play of curiosity that continues as we read *The Cantos*, a poem devoted to the celebration of a division; and Pound cannot legislate this curiosity out of existence. It contributes to the judgment one passes on the poem, as an imitation of reality, as a source of 'renewing' reality.

If this analysis of the 'effect' of reading *The Cantos* is just, what is that effect? One of freezing inertia. Shall we say that the will (much less the intelligence) is not moved on the terms that Pound permits and presents in his poem? What the poem presents us is a sharp perception of hate or the hateful balanced by no more than an omnibus, cultivated, eclectic perception of good. This good, upon acquaintance, becomes (for all the specificity with which it is revealed) as vague and unsatisfying as 'The Good' in some nineteenth century systems. It may occur to us that Pound is expecting a great miracle indeed from his poem; for nowhere, to date, do we find a society that resisted evil, tramped it to earth, on the basis of an omnibus, undiscriminating perception of good. The most, in this sort, that we find to date is a poem, Ezra Pound's *The Cantos*.

It is a poem—this study has made clear—for which we should be grateful. It is the record of a negative criticism of our society that we should not ignore. It is the record of a real (if ultimately somewhat frustrated) struggle with the interrelated artistic and political problems which our period presented one poet. But not only one poet. For these same problems of renewing the techniques of poetry, of renewing the society which poetry serves, will become intimately ours the more we think of the mode of existence, of solution, they had when they were Pound's. However qualified our assent to the special answers Pound worked out, we know that Pound has a claim to great distinction—and not just because he has bent his vision on these problems and no others for a great many years. We may feel that an intransigent nominalist pose is more confining than Pound believed; we may think—possibly thanks to his negative demonstration—that making things new requires a more sensitive and various response to experience than *The Cantos* records. We may decide that at certain points Pound was self-deceived. But we cannot believe that central to his career is an intent to deceive us. We should see by now that the 'truth' about Ezra Pound and *The Cantos* is—wholly or in part—the truth about matters that ought to be our first concern: the estate of poetry in our culture, the role of language in that culture, the sort of belief needful if that culture is to survive and unfold, the conditions under which belief of any sort is arrived at. This is the gift which Ezra Pound offers the country which he left; it should countervail much that is urged against him.

INDEX

INDEX